The MULTICULTURAL *Mindset*

JOYCELYN DAVID

The
MULTICULTURAL
Mindset

DRIVING BUSINESS GROWTH
IN A BORDERLESS ERA

Advantage | Books

Published by Advantage Books, Charleston, South Carolina.
An imprint of Advantage Media.

ADVANTAGE is a registered trademark, and the Advantage colophon is a trademark of Advantage Media Group, Inc.

Printed in the United States of America.

10 9 8 7 6 5 4 3 2 1

ISBN: 979-8-89188-120-4 (Paperback)
ISBN: 979-8-89188-121-1 (eBook)

Library of Congress Control Number: 2025906667

Book design by Megan Elger.

This publication is designed to provide accurate and authoritative information in regard to the subject matter covered. It is sold with the understanding that the publisher is not engaged in rendering legal, accounting, or other professional services. If legal advice or other expert assistance is required, the services of a competent professional person should be sought.

Advantage Books is an imprint of Advantage Media Group. Advantage Media helps busy entrepreneurs, CEOs, and leaders write and publish a book to grow their business and become the authority in their field. Advantage authors comprise an exclusive community of industry professionals, idea-makers, and thought leaders. For more information go to **advantagemedia.com**.

To my grandparents, Marcial and Teresita, and my parents, Jose and Restita:

Your courageous journey from the Philippines opened new possibilities for our family in Canada. Your willingness to step beyond the familiar taught me that true growth lies outside our comfort zones.

To my husband, Abe:

For being the fish to my chips and loving me exactly as I am. *Kaluguran daka.*

To Lorenzo, my son and miracle:

You inspire me daily, and being your mom is my greatest joy.

To my sisters, Marites and Anita:

For keeping your Ate grounded and real.

To my extended Espiritu and David families:

Across Canada, the United States, and the Philippines—you've shown me the strength of cultural bonds.

And finally, to everyone navigating between cultures, to those who've questioned where they belong, to those who've wondered if they're "enough," to those bridging multiple worlds:

This book is for you. Your ability to navigate multiple realities isn't a weakness—it's your superpower.

Own it.

CONTENTS

ACKNOWLEDGMENTS

I want to thank the following people, without whom this book wouldn't have been possible.

The AVCommunications team: past and present employees who bring the Multicultural Mindset to life daily; cofounders Marvi Yap and Anna Maramba for their pioneering vision; and the Leadership Team, Shaharyar Irfan, Shirley Leng, Hassan Iqbal, Tonia Au, and Ulyssis Enrico, for being extraordinary partners in our mission toward inclusive marketing.

The TULONG Technologies start-up team: Chamanvir Kaur, Binod Banjara, Meet Soni, and Ritika Shah.

My Western Union mentors: Brian Fox, Juan Carlos Blanco, and Chito Gonzalez.

Advisors, industry experts, community advocates, and contributors: Declan Ramsaran, Pangea Family Office; Alina Martin and Chadi Azzi, BDC Canada; Joy Chen, The Multicultural Leadership Institute; Nadia Niccoli, Diageo Canada; Nick Noorani, Immigrant Networks; Grace Tong and Megan Miller, Ipsos Canada; and Anna Patrizio, Dr. Eileen de Villa, Honourable Minister Rechie Valdez, and Rosary Escaño, Filipina Women's Network Canada.

The POCAM SteerCo and board members: Aleena Mazhar, Chino Nnadi, Erik dela Cruz, Gavin Barrett, Ishma Alexander-Huet, Julian Franklin, Justin Senior, Natalie Bomberry, Deyra Jaye Fontaine, Matthew Tsang, Ken Saint-Eloy, and Mark Rutledge.

INTRODUCTION

"The real voyage of discovery consists not in seeking
new landscapes, but in having new eyes."
–Marcel Proust

Two moments, separated by decades, taught me the power of
culture in our rapidly evolving world.

The first came in 1989. I was in sixth grade, clutching a
container of sago—the Filipino version of what would later
become known globally as "bubble tea." As part of our "Share Your
Culture" project, we were bringing food from our cultural backgrounds. Little Joycelyn was excited to share one of her absolute
favourite treats: sweet brown sugar syrup with gelatinous pearls
floating in it.

In 1989, bubble tea hadn't yet become the global phenomenon it is today. You couldn't find it on every street corner like
you can now. My classmates recoiled at what looked to them like
strange floating "eyeballs." Their laughter sent me running from the
classroom in tears while my teacher attempted to lecture them about
respecting other cultures.

The impact lingered. I stopped drinking sago, denying myself
something I loved because of shame—until years later, in college,

1

when I witnessed non-Asian students casually sipping bubble tea between classes. That moment crystallized something profound: It took twenty-five years for this food to become accepted in the mainstream. How many other cultural treasures are we missing out on because we're not ready to understand them?

Fast-forward to July 2024. I'm standing on stage at San Diego Comic Con, moderating a panel about representation in comics. The lineup includes industry veterans of Filipino background like myself: Whilce Portacio, revered as essentially the "Stan Lee of the Filipino community"; technology veterans Sharleen Dee Sy and Cecilia Lim; senior comics publisher Hank Kanalz; and apl.de.ap, world-renowned musician and cofounder of the Black Eyed Peas.

During the panel, apl.de.ap shared how his adoptive American parents ensured he maintained connection with his cultural heritage, even arranging friendships with other children of colour—including will.i.am, who would later become his Black Eyed Peas bandmate. This intentional cultural bridging shaped not only his personal journey but also his creative vision.

THE POWER OF CULTURAL UNDERSTANDING

These stories bookend a transformation in how we think about culture—from something to be ashamed of to something to be celebrated. But we're not just dealing with changing attitudes. We're facing demographic shifts that are reshaping our world:

- By 2041, up to 34 percent of Canadians will be foreign born.[1]

---

1   Colin R. Singer, "Immigrants and Their Children Set to Dominate Canada Population by 2041," immigration.ca, September 9, 2022, https://immigration.ca/immigrants-and-their-children-set-to-dominate-canada-population-by-2041/.

- Multicultural consumers command over \$5.6 trillion in buying power in the United States.[2]

- Companies with above-average diversity on their leadership teams report 19 percent higher innovation revenue than those with below-average diversity.[3]

Yet many organizations still struggle to navigate this new reality. As both a CEO and entrepreneur leading two companies in Canada, I've witnessed firsthand how cultural understanding—or its absence—can make or break

- team dynamics,

- customer relationships,

- market opportunities, and

- innovation capabilities.

INTRODUCING THE MULTICULTURAL MINDSET

This challenge led me to develop what I call the Multicultural Mindset—a framework for understanding and engaging with cultural differences that goes beyond surface-level diversity. To measure this capability, I've created the Multicultural Quotient (MQ)—a tool that, like IQ for cognitive intelligence or EQ for emotional intelligence, helps assess and develop cultural competency.

2   Megan Poinski, "Growth Depends on Marketing to Multicultural Audiences," *Forbes*, May 1, 2024, https://www.forbes.com/sites/cmo/2024/05/01/growth-depends-on-marketing-to-multicultural-audiences/.

3   Rocío Lorenzo et al., "How Diverse Leadership Teams Boost Innovation," BCG Global, January 23, 2018, https://www.bcg.com/publications/2018/how-diverse-leadership-teams-boost-innovation.

You can find the MQ tool at this link:

In an era when global business faces both unprecedented opportunities and complex challenges, the ability to navigate cultural landscapes has moved from a nice-to-have skill to a critical business imperative.

I'm saddened to see governments and organizations stepping back diversity initiatives. The world is not colour blind, and the fundamental need to operate effectively across cultural boundaries has only intensified.

This is where the Multicultural Mindset framework and the MQ tool offer a fresh, business-focused approach.

My book is my gift to those who stand at the abyss looking out, wondering "What can I do?" You can look to your own mindset to build core skills needed for success in our colourful and interconnected world.

Think of it as your internal GPS for navigating global markets—it's not about where you're from but how effectively you can operate anywhere. This mindset encompasses two critical elements: first, an acute awareness of rapidly evolving cultural dynamics in our interconnected world, and second, the capacity to navigate, empathize with, and relate to cultures beyond your own experience.

The Multicultural Mindset isn't just another business concept; it's a crucial operating system for today's global marketplace. By measuring and developing MQ, organizations can build the practical skills needed to thrive in an interconnected world, regardless of political climate or social trends. This isn't about where we stand on political or social issues; it's about how effectively we can better understand those who are different from us in order to operate across borders, build international partnerships, and capture opportunities in the global marketplace.

WHAT YOU'LL LEARN

In this book, we'll explore both the Multicultural Mindset and the MQ. We'll cover

1. a systematic approach to developing your Multicultural Mindset,

2. tools for measuring and improving your MQ,

3. practical strategies for implementing cultural intelligence,

4. real-world case studies of success and failure, and

5. future-focused approaches for the AI Era.

Through eight chapters, we'll explore

1. the nature of our Multicultural Multiverse,

2. how to develop a Multicultural Mindset,

3. making multiculturalism mainstream,

4. going beyond surface-level understanding,

5. overcoming cultural resistance,

6. building meaningful connections,

7. creating inclusive organizations, and

8. preparing for an AI-powered future.

THE JOURNEY AHEAD

As you begin this journey with me, it's important to understand that developing a Multicultural Mindset isn't about checking boxes or following a rigid formula; it's about cultivating a way of thinking that allows you to thrive in our increasingly interconnected world. Whether you're

- a business leader seeking to build effective, diverse teams,

- an entrepreneur wanting to expand your market reach,

- a professional navigating global workspaces, or

- an individual hoping to better understand our changing world,

the principles and practices in this book will help you develop the cultural intelligence needed for success in the Multicultural Era.

WHY I WROTE THIS BOOK

My career in marketing stemmed from my graduate studies in communications and cultural studies, and, in hindsight, my desire to find my place in the world as a Filipina who couldn't speak her own language fluently. I've worked across borders, with thousands of employees in both global and multinational settings, and won awards in business, philanthropy, and marketing—including being named one of the Most Influential Filipinas in the World.

People often ask me, "As a woman and a visible minority throughout your career, what has been your key to success? How did you break through the ceiling? How did you manage the racism and the misogyny?"

My answer is always a version of this: I honed my skills in cross-cultural communication, understanding through experience, and I developed a Multicultural Mindset. That, for me, is *the* key to success in today's global world of business and community.

THE STAKES HAVE NEVER BEEN HIGHER

Today's reality shows how far we've come. When I say I'm Filipina, people understand the context and recognize the unique identity and culture it represents. But we're at a critical juncture:

- AI is reshaping how we interact.

- Global migration is transforming communities.

- Technology is accelerating cultural exchange.

- Traditional boundaries are dissolving.

These changes create both opportunities and challenges:

- For businesses: the chance to reach new markets and tap diverse talent

- For leaders: the need to build truly inclusive organizations

- For individuals: the opportunity to thrive in multicultural environments

- For society: the imperative to foster genuine understanding

A PERSONAL INVITATION

Drawing from the lessons of my career, I am sharing the Multicultural Mindset framework so you can embrace its benefits for your own journey. This book represents everything I have learned over twenty years of collective conversations on nuance, understanding, and empathy—the bedrocks of cross-cultural communication.

With everything moving so fast, this book is my invitation to you to slow down and look deeper. And you might just find that cultivating this mindset has another benefit as well: It can be part of the lifelong journey to finding your own sense of identity and purpose in our multicultural world.

Imagine how different the world could be if people were being taught how to empathize, understand, and communicate more effectively with a multicultural lens. Are you ready to be a part of that new world?

Then let's begin our journey into the Multicultural Mindset. We'll start at the very beginning ...

CHAPTER 1

THE MULTICULTURAL MULTIVERSE

"Cultural intelligence is a lifelong journey; we should never stop learning and adapting to new cultural contexts."

–Erin Meyer

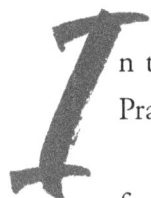

*I*n the beginning, there was a Filipina from the Canadian Prairies.

Imagine long winters, fields of wheat, and rolling boreal forests blending into the wide skies of northern Alberta. And imagine a territory settled primarily by immigrants from Eastern European countries who were attracted to the free land and were skilled as farmers and able to survive the harsh winter conditions. And imagine me, a chubby Filipina, who looked around and saw nobody—outside of her parents and a small church community—who looked like her.

I had a lot of Ukrainian, Polish, and Italian friends growing up in Edmonton, Alberta. This changed when a small group of Filipinos migrated to Edmonton and put down roots in our local church. My mom found community in the other Filipino families, and I found fast friends who had a shared lived experience. Claire, Cathy, and

Bernie were my besties, and we grew up together, singing Paula Abdul and Tiffany on karaoke machines that had not yet become mainstream in Canada.

Despite our shared Filipino background, none of us spoke Tagalog (the main Filipino dialect) at home. Interestingly, this was actually quite accepted among the elders of our community. Later in life, when I asked my mom why, she explained that it was a conscious decision—and one many immigrant parents make. We didn't speak Filipino at home because she didn't want me to have an accent. She didn't want me to be pushed even further into the "other" category. I wouldn't learn Tagalog until I was a teenager and sought it out myself. Growing up not learning or speaking Tagalog always contributed to my feeling of being "less" Filipina because I didn't have the language skills.

For all these reasons, I understood what it was like to be "other" from a very young age. I didn't consciously identify as Filipina because the community was very small, apart from my three friends and my parents. I thought of myself as a Canadian, living in the Prairies. And yet, throughout my childhood, people would ask me what I was, where I was from. "I'm Canadian," I would say. "I'm from Alberta."

"But where are you *from*?" they would insist. I didn't understand; I was born in Canada. I now know they were referring to my ethnicity rather than where I was actually born. That was how they wanted to categorize me, how they wanted to place me in the world. But the fact is, I was both; I was Filipina *and* I was Canadian.

In fact, Canadian policy itself supported this dual identity. In the 1970s, Canada implemented a multicultural policy normalizing and clearly communicating—and thereby celebrating—hyphenated identities. In the United States, when you look at the available boxes to check, you are White, Black, Hispanic, Asian, Other, etc. In Canada, those boxes are much more multicultural as a starting point. This is our normal. There is a codified acceptance of the hyphenated, multicultural identity.

Because you *can* have more than one identity; in fact, we all do have more than one identity. I instinctively understood this as a child, but it was in college that I really began to dig into what exactly this "multiculturalism" means—not just for myself, but for us all, as individuals and as a global society.

WHAT IS MULTICULTURALISM?

Multiculturalism is not a new idea or label—but it is fairly recent. Although the idea of people from disparate groups living together goes back millennia, the concept of multiculturalism took root in modern society less than one hundred years ago.

Our modern conception of multiculturalism was formulated in Canada in the 1960s by the Royal Commission on Bilingualism and Biculturalism, and on their recommendation, multiculturalism within a bilingual framework was officially adopted as Canadian federal policy in 1971 by Prime Minister Pierre Trudeau (father of former Prime Minister Justin Trudeau).[4] The idea behind these policies was to honour the diversity found in Canada's society, from language to religion to ethnicity.

Canada was the first country in the world to adopt such a policy as an official act—and this played a big role in families like mine choosing to immigrate here. It also led to the Canadian Multiculturalism Act of 1988, which "serves as a legislative framework for

---

4   Daniel Meister et al., "Canadian Multiculturalism Policy, 1971," Canadian Museum of Immigration at Pier 21, accessed August 10, 2024, https://pier21.ca/research/immigration-history/canadian-multiculturalism-policy-1971.

promoting diversity, equality, and inclusion in Canada, recognizing multiculturalism as a defining characteristic of Canadian identity."[5]

The objectives of the Act, as laid out on the official website of the Canadian government, are[6]

- recognizing and preserving the multicultural heritage of Canadians,

- promoting the full and equitable participation of individuals and communities of all origins in the continuing evolution and shaping of all aspects of Canadian society,

- assisting individuals and communities of all origins to eliminate barriers to their participation in Canadian society, and

- assuring that all individuals receive equal treatment and equal protection under the law while respecting and valuing their diversity.

The Act emphasizes the importance of cultural diversity as a fundamental characteristic of Canadian identity and promotes the idea that all Canadians should have the opportunity to preserve, enhance, and share their cultural heritage. It encourages the government to support initiatives that foster intercultural understanding and respect. Overall, the Act serves as a legislative framework for the promotion and protection of multiculturalism in Canada.

For more than fifty years, Canada has embraced multiculturalism, in contrast to the mindsets and policies of nations that emphasize assimilation or integration—or nationalism. Multiculturalism stands in contrast to nationalism, which dictates that we are all the same, we are all human,

---

5   "About the Canadian Multiculturalism Act," Government of Canada, June 3, 2024, https://www.canada.ca/en/canadian-heritage/services/about-multiculturalism-anti-racism/about-act.html.

6   Ibid.

we are all Canadian (or American or whatever nationality applies to you). This may sound like a great idea, but the reality is that we are not all exactly the same. We are not just one; we are also many. Nationalism tends to create politicized and racialized lines as well as an "us versus them" mentality. Multiculturalism emphasizes the many in the "we."

Multiculturalism began as a policy to help preserve particular cultural practices in the private sphere. Our conception of multiculturalism is one that encourages people to contribute to and participate in society as a whole. It is a social philosophy that identifies and gives value to all of the different types of cultural and ethnic groups contained within a country, area, region, or any other place that's considered a society. Multiculturalism is about appreciating the diversity of the many facets that make up a culture and wanting everyone to coexist with mutual respect for each other.

EARLY FRAMEWORKS

In the course of my studies, I encountered two great thinkers who paved the way for how we think about multiculturalism and set me

on a path to codify my own thinking about multiculturalism: Geert Hofstede and Erin Meyer.

Hofstede and Cultural Dimensions

In his 1980 book *Culture's Consequences*, Hofstede mapped out the different dimensions of culture that make us unique.[7] His model includes six dimensions of culture: Power Distance, Uncertainty Avoidance, Individualism/Collectivism, Masculinity/Femininity, Long-/Short-Term Orientation, and Indulgence/Restraint.

Over time, similar concepts have been adapted into the well-known and widely used culture wheel—a visual representation of the different elements that make up a culture.

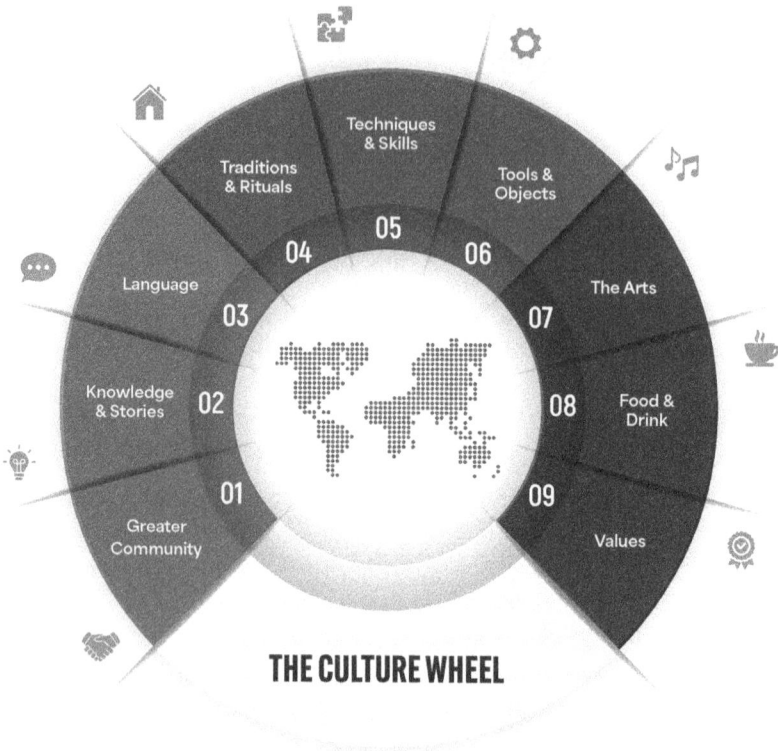

THE CULTURE WHEEL

---

7   Geert Hofstede, *Culture's Consequences: Comparing Values, Behaviors, Institutions and Organizations Across Nations* (SAGE, 2001).

The culture wheel shows culture as the sum of all these elements. One interesting thing to note is that, in this breakdown, culture has nothing to do with your ethnicity or background. Skin colour is not even a facet of culture on the culture wheel. It has to do with the inputs of lived experience and knowledge that you encounter, from your greater community to the language, traditions, or food you share.

For example, I have a very good friend who is Canadian, of mixed European ancestry, but was raised in Hong Kong. She speaks Mandarin fluently and has lived more of her life in Hong Kong than in North America. She married a Japanese expat she met in Hong Kong, and they now have a beautiful family that is multiracial through and through. If you look at her, however, you might jump to conclusions based on her appearance. And therein lies the challenge: We only see what we see, and culture runs deeper than surface level, beyond skin colour, race, or ethnicity.

We have to challenge our own misconceptions. We should be looking for and celebrating those points of intersection. Looking at any of these elements in isolation can be dangerous. It can lead to stereotypes such as "all Chinese people speak Mandarin," which is not true—many Chinese people speak Cantonese, not Mandarin! It is dangerous to say culture equals just one of these things on the wheel.

These misconceptions find their way into business, marketing, and everyday interactions in today's global world. For example, language is one of the spokes of the wheel, but it is not the only one. And yet, too many of my clients in my day-to-day job think "multicultural marketing" is just translating marketing into different languages. Yes, language is a very important piece of the expression of culture. But it is only one aspect of culture and should be considered in context with all aspects of the culture wheel.

Of course, it is hard for brands to understand all of these cultural elements—and this is often where marketing agencies, cultural consultants, and diversity specialists can play a role. Cultural experts, insiders, or agencies can help bridge the knowledge gap and seek out the diverse inputs and perspectives that are a cornerstone of multiculturalism. One cannot build this alone!

The many dimensions that make up a culture also mean there are multiple ways to get to know it. You may not be able to speak the language, but you can participate in a tradition such as Lunar New Year. This experience gives you access to the culture wheel without having to master every element of it.

Erin Meyer and the Culture Map

Erin Meyer, a corporate trainer for global companies, built on Hofstede's work in her 2014 book *The Culture Map*.[8] In her work, Meyer was looking to understand different learning styles for big, global companies. She looked at Hofstede's framework from a global business perspective, exploring how to use Hofstede's concepts to help employees in different countries communicate and work effectively with each other.

Meyer was focused on how global companies work together—how workers in the Paris office and the Singapore office could effectively communicate. As our world becomes more interconnected, such interactions are becoming more frequent. While cultural diversity can inspire creativity and drive innovation, it can also lead to confusion and miscommunication. This highlights the growing importance of effective cross-cultural communication for success in today's globalized society.

Meyer identified eight cultural dimensions that impact communication and interaction in a business context:

---

8   Erin Meyer, *The Culture Map: Breaking Through the Invisible Boundaries of Global Business* (PublicAffairs, 2014).

8 DIMENSIONS OF CULTURE IMPACTING BUSINESS

"Book Summary—The Culture Map: Breaking Through the Invisible Boundaries of Global Business," Readingraphics (blog), June 30, 2024, https://readingraphics.com/book-summary-the-culture-map-erin-meyer/.

- **Communicating**: low-context (direct, precise, and clearly expressed) versus high-context (multilayered and nuanced, requires reading between the lines)

- **Evaluating**: direct (given openly, even in front of others) versus indirect (packaged nicely to take the edge off and usually given in private) negative feedback

- **Persuading**: principles-first (thinking big and starting with theory to create solutions) versus applications-first (starting with the solution, followed by theoretical discussions)

- **Leading**: egalitarian (leader's role is to facilitate rather than manage; greater equality between manager and subordinate) versus hierarchical (greater distance between manager and subordinate; leader has authority and is clearly distinguished from colleagues)

- **Deciding**: consensual (involving a high number of participants and feedback) versus top-down (made by authority and passed down to lower levels)

- **Trusting**: task-based (based on competence) versus relationship-based (based on getting to know a person)

- **Disagreeing**: confrontational (debate is considered necessary and appropriate) versus avoids confrontation (debate seen as a disruption)

- **Scheduling**: linear-time (tasks completed chronologically; focus on order and punctuality) versus flexible-time (goals and deadlines often changing)

COMMUNICATING: LOW-CONTEXT VS HIGH-CONTEXT CULTURES

COMMUNICATION

Low Context
Messages are explicit, clear, direct, and often repeated.

High Context
Messages are nuanced, layered, with many subtle signals.

US	Netherlands	Finland		Spain	Italy	Singapore	Iran	China	Japan
Australia	Germany	Denmark	Poland	Brazil	Mexico	France	India	Kenya	Korea
Canada		UK		Argentina	Peru	Russia	Saudi Arabia		Indonesia

"Book Summary—The Culture Map: Breaking Through the Invisible Boundaries of Global Business," Readingraphics (blog), June 30, 2024, https://readingraphics.com/book-summary-the-culture-map-erin-meyer/.

Hofstede's and Meyer's work—along with the growing body of scholarly and industry-focused writings on the topic of multiculturalism—have inspired my career as an entrepreneur and leader and provided the jumping-off point for my own framework.

My focus is on zooming out to all the citizens of the world who can now embrace this perspective, whether you work at a global company or not. We're taking this framework outside the business world and thinking about how it can apply to individuals in a global, borderless world—which, in turn, can benefit professionals, managers, and leaders of tomorrow.

WELCOME TO THE MULTICULTURAL MULTIVERSE

When you look at the culture wheel, it can be easy to imagine every culture as its own sphere, its own little universe, containing all those elements from the wheel. This is reflected in the work of both Hofstede and Meyer, who studied cultures as isolated entities, even when, in Meyer's case, cultures were interacting in a business setting. But the reality of 2024 is a hyperconnected world moving at the speed of clicks and likes where these spheres don't exist in isolation. Instead, they exist in a multiverse of spheres existing alongside—and frequently colliding with—each other, like bumper cars but without a driver.

In this Multicultural Multiverse, nothing is static, and like in all things, not all of the spheres are equal. There are dominant cultures. There are smaller subcultures. All of these cultures, all of these attitudes, beliefs, customs, and behaviours, are intersecting like cells, oscillating in the universe and vibrating with kinetic energy. They are converging in the space that we call society and intersecting at what I call cultural nodes. A cultural node is a point of intersection in our globally connected community. Diverse societies have multiple points or multiple cultural nodes.

MULTIVERSE OF CULTURES
Always On & Intersecting

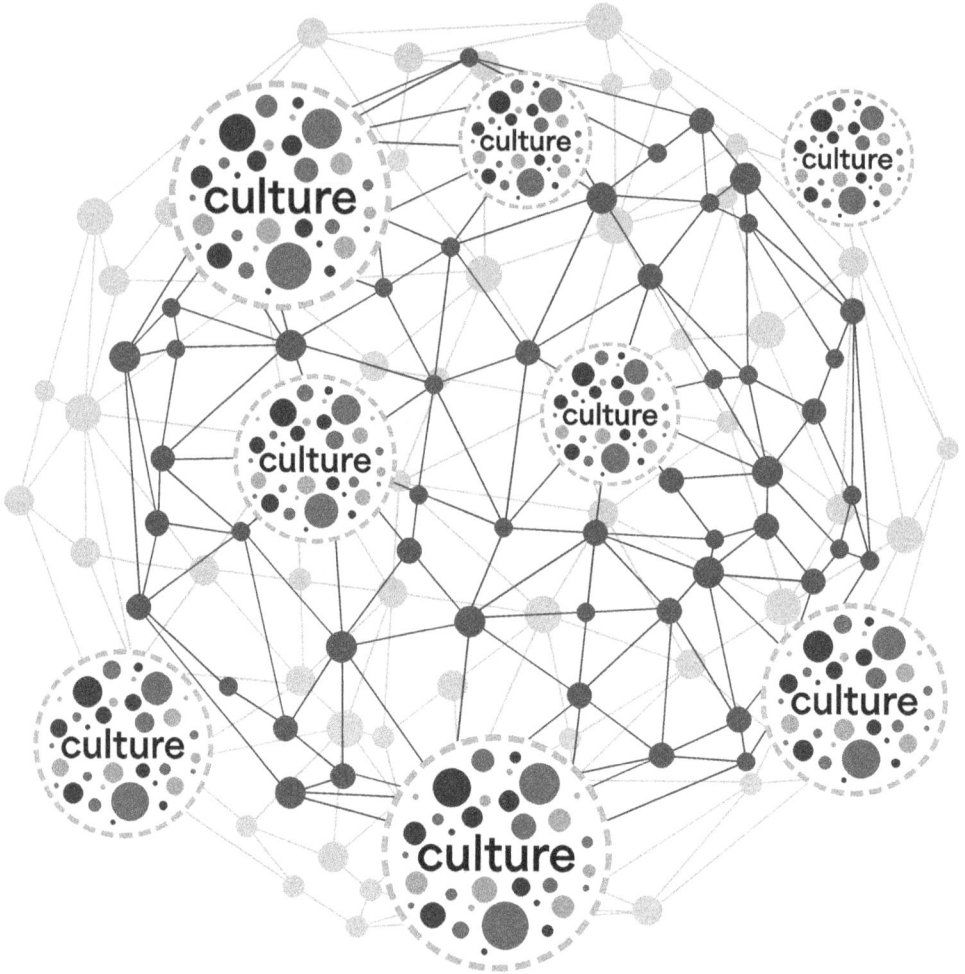

So, what happens when all these things collide, when they intersect? First of all, it disrupts tunnel vision.

From Tunnel Vision to Cultural Fluency

"In building cultural fluency, get comfortable
being uncomfortable."
–Joycelyn David

Tunnel vision often refers to a narrow or limited perspective, where an individual becomes so focused on a specific task, goal, or problem that they fail to see the broader context or consider alternative viewpoints. In a multicultural society, this can lead to missing opportunities to build cultural fluency.

Tunnel vision is not all bad; it can help build a strong sense of focus, self, and identity, fostering a positive sense of personal or community identity. However, tunnel vision only includes one's own culture, customs, or language.

In his book *Tribal: How the Cultural Instincts That Divide Us Can Help Bring Us Together*, the "tribalism" Michael Morris writes about is very similar to this idea of tunnel vision. Morris writes about how ancient humans evolved to have the survival instinct to form insular groups as a means of protection, which still influences behaviour today. This tribalism fosters a sense of belonging and solidarity within groups, based on race, religion, politics, nationality, or other shared identities. Unfortunately, Morris writes, this tribalism can often result in an antagonistic "us versus them" mentality—"us" being everyone who is within your cultural sphere and "them" being everyone in cultural spheres outside your own.[9]

Visually, tunnel vision might look something like this: a rectangle built up of these different blocks of culture.

---

9   Michael Morris, *Tribal: How the Cultural Instincts That Divide Us Can Help Bring Us Together* (Penguin, 2024).

TUNNEL VISION

BUILDING MQ
Widening Viewpoints

Personalized &
Preferred

Learned CXP
cultural experience

Lived XP

Roots

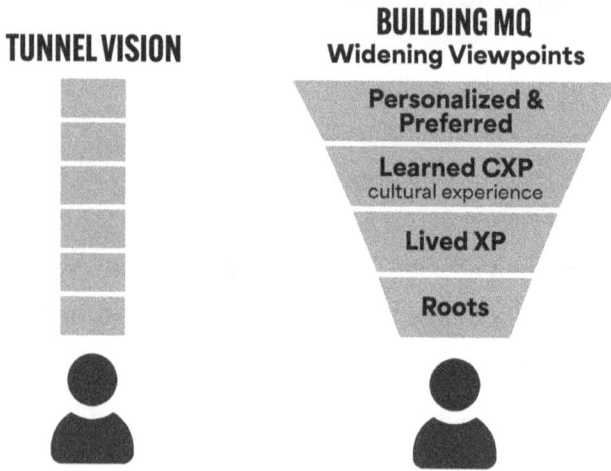

This rectangle is pretty much how I grew up for most of my life as a Filipina in the Prairies of Canada. Each block made up a part of my sense of identity. But, as I became more exposed to the world through work, travel, and study, my worldview expanded beyond that rectangle of blocks and into something more like a pyramid. The rectangle forms my roots, and my lived experiences through which I have encountered and gotten to know other cultures build on that, shaping it into a flourishing larger worldview.

Growing up in a multicultural country gave me more access to cultural fluency, which in turn allowed me to view multiculturalism as normal rather than controversial. Increased cultural fluency provides the ability to navigate across the Multicultural Multiverse of cultural nodes that are constantly in movement.

Les Roches, one of the world's leading schools for global hospitality, defines cultural fluency as:

> … the ability to move comfortably among cultures from the individual cultural wheel or sphere of one's community to the cultural sphere of another. Increased cultural fluency

refers to one's ability to understand, communicate and engage with people from different cultural backgrounds. This fluency goes well beyond just spoken language; it's also the ability to recognize and understand the context of different behavioural norms and engage appropriately.

Cultural fluency involves being aware of what's considered appropriate etiquette around the world—from body language to physical contact to eye contact. It means having next-level emotional intelligence, being sensitive to cultural nuances, and being adaptable in your interactions with individuals from other cultures.[10]

According to Les Roches, cultural fluency continues to be one of the top employability skills in demand. In other words, if you have cultural fluency, you are more likely to get hired!

So, how do you increase your cultural fluency? How can you best access and experience and have a widening viewpoint that is rooted in cultural fluency?

It starts with consciously seeking people and experiences outside your community. If you don't do this, you will never escape your own cultural sphere and will end up spinning around in place like a hamster on a wheel. This is how we end up with division, with ignorance, with people believing in stereotypes about those who are different from themselves.

We all naturally have that tunnel vision about what we know, what we have experienced, and what we are aware of. The best way to expand this view is through shared experiences and experiencing new things.

10　Camille Prulhiere, "Why Cross-Cultural Fluency Is a Top Skill for Employability," *Les Roches* (blog), February 8, 2022, https://lesroches.edu/blog/cross-cultural-fluency/.

On this subject, my good friend, entrepreneur, and author Nick Noorani, has a lot to say. Born in Mumbai, India, Nick came to Canada in 1998 with a world of international experience in advertising and marketing in three countries. Despite this, he faced many challenges in his new Canadian home, and he noticed that many other immigrants were also struggling.

In 2000, Nick coauthored the hugely successful book *Arrival Survival Canada*, subsequently published by Oxford University Press.[11] This led to his creation of *Canadian Immigrant* magazine, Canada's first national magazine for all immigrants, launched in 2004. In 2007, Nick sold the magazine to Star Media Group, a division of Toronto Star Newspapers Ltd., and continued in his position as publisher.

I had the pleasure of hearing Nick deliver his "Seven Success Secrets for Canadian Immigrants" program live in Edmonton, which really left a mark on me. In brief, the seven secrets are as follows:[12]

1. **Learn the language:** Mastering English or French is critical for communication and integration into Canadian society.

2. **Stay positive:** Maintaining optimism in the face of challenges is essential for long-term success, even when facing setbacks such as difficulty finding employment.

3. **Understand Canadian workplace culture:** Learn the nuances of how the Canadian work environment operates to better navigate professional interactions.

4. **Have a plan B:** Always be ready with alternative career options or strategies, as flexibility can lead to new opportunities.

---

11 Naeem Noorani and Sabrina Noorani, *Arrival Survival Canada: A Handbook for New Immigrants* (Oxford University Press, 2008).

12 "7 Success Secrets for Canadian Immigrants," Live & Learn, July 11, 2016, https://livelearn.ca/article/community-circles/7-success-secrets-for-canadian-immigrants/.

5. **Move out of ethnic silos:** Expanding your social circle beyond your ethnic community will help with integration and foster new professional relationships.

6. **Take risks:** Embrace new challenges, such as career changes or learning new skills, to fully engage with life in Canada.

7. **Engage in volunteering and networking:** Volunteering offers a way to gain Canadian experience, while networking opens up job opportunities that may not be advertised.

The first secret was actually what my parents enforced with our family. We spoke English exclusively at home, and the Tagalog language was nearly lost. Nick's hard advice to immigrants was to get out of your bubble and start learning the language of the place you call home. Experience the culture of your new home.

"I could have just stayed in India if I wanted to eat Indian food and have all Indian friends," Nick said in the speech I heard him deliver.

"I came to Canada to learn more and new things. This is the essence and resilience of immigrants." This was very controversial for someone in the Indian community to say twenty years ago!

Nick's very sage advice has always stuck with me—and it's why he and I continued to collaborate on projects over the years. His advice and bravery helped me out of my own tunnel vision and led me to develop a stronger understanding of the plight of immigrants. In fact, in many ways, my parents' decision not to teach me Tagalog was aligned with Nick's number one secret; they did it to help me survive and thrive in Canada.

My parents weren't the only ones to instinctively follow Nick's advice. My husband moved to Canada when he was a young teenager, and his sister gave him the same advice Nick gives: Go meet other Canadians. She suggested he do this by finding a job. So, he got a job at McDonald's—but all the staff were Filipino! They ended up speaking Tagalog all the time, and it didn't do anything to get him outside his bubble. Eventually, he changed jobs and grew a wider circle of friends, colleagues, and acquaintances—which eventually led to him meeting me in senior year of high school (but we'll talk more about my husband and family later).

RECOGNIZING YOUR OWN TUNNEL VISION

There have been plenty of painful moments in my life when I have faced a realization about how narrow my worldview is. Those moments stick with you!

One formative experience of needing to widen my tunnel vision was when I was fourteen and went to the Philippines for the first time. Until that point, I had only ever heard about the land of my parents' birth. So, there I was, a pampered fourteen-year-old kid from Canada, with no understanding of how life was there.

The family members we were visiting in the Philippines were very poor. They lived out in the countryside, without a flush toilet or even running water. Living in Canada, I was not prepared for the heat and humidity of the Philippines. I felt like I was dying. On my very first day, I stood in the makeshift bathroom—just sheets of scrap metal with little wooden planks to hold them up along with a makeshift door, a makeshift toilet with no lid on it, and a big bucket of water. I was so hot, I took scoop after scoop of water out of that bucket, pouring it over my head. It felt so good! It was so hot, and the cool water was so refreshing that I pretty much emptied the bucket. It felt like the best bath of my life. Afterward, I got dressed and went about my day.

A couple hours later, I saw about twenty little kids in shorts and T-shirts and flip-flops, probably no older than eight or nine, carrying buckets of water into the makeshift bathroom to refill the big bucket of water I had depleted. I started following them and realized they were filling the smaller buckets at a water pump that was two kilometres away and then carrying the full buckets of water all the way back to the bathroom. And they had to do this because the entitled kid from Canada had used more water in a single bath than the entire family used in a week. You can bet, after that, I only used one small bucket of water for my baths and always helped the kids refill the big bucket!

This was a huge cultural shock for me in terms of poverty and entitlement. In terms of the Multicultural Quotient (MQ), at this point in my life, I was definitely MQ Red (we'll get into what that means in the next chapter). It was also a cultural shock to be among so many people who looked like me. I had never seen so many Filipinos in my life! Everyone was Filipino! I felt as though I was in *The Twilight Zone*. Everyone looked like me, but I felt completely like a foreigner. That feeling of being a foreigner in the land of my parents' birth—my cultural homeland—stuck with me. I am Filipina, but I'm also not.

This was when I first truly understood that culture is not about how you look or your ethnic background. I was of the same ethnic background as my family in the Philippines, but the cultural differences were huge.

I think this is a common experience for immigrants, for the children of immigrants, for people with hybrid backgrounds—so many of us feel as though we don't really *belong* anywhere. But as the world becomes increasingly multicultural, we are starting to approach a world where everyone belongs everywhere. In a true Multicultural Multiverse, there are no borders.

Later in life, I would continue to have similar moments in the workplace and in the boardroom—both of experiencing my own tunnel vision and of confronting the tunnel vision of others—but this was my first experience seeing how important it is to be understanding of those who are different from ourselves; those who might feel isolated because they are not part of the majority culture in a given space; those whose way of life might be very different from mine. It showed me the importance of examining my own version of what is right and wrong and viewing things from different perspectives.

There is always something to be learned in having empathy for those who are not like you—whether it is a different cultural or subcultural group, a different gender, a different ethnicity, or a different social class. The question is, if you find yourself in a situation like this, will you take that knowledge and add it to your toolkit, use it to inform your mindset for the future?

Getting out of your bubble is at the heart of building the most essential tool for the modern era: a Multicultural Mindset.

KEY TAKEAWAYS

→ Our modern concept of multiculturalism is less than one hundred years old, but it has been codified into policy—the first instance being the federal policy of multiculturalism adopted in Canada in 1971—and mapped out by scholars such as Geert Hofstede and Erin Meyer.

→ We are living in a Multicultural Multiverse, where spheres of culture are oscillating and intersecting at cultural nodes.

→ When spheres intersect or collide, it breaks us out of tunnel vision and opens a pathway away from tribalism and toward cultural fluency.

CHAPTER 2

INTRODUCING THE MULTICULTURAL MINDSET

"Our cultural strength has always been derived from
our diversity of understanding and experience."

–Yo-Yo Ma

Let me share something that took me years to fully understand: Our world is so much more fascinating when you have a Multicultural Mindset.

Think of it like one of those amazing Filipino desserts I love—you know, the one Anthony Bourdain described as a "technicolour concoction," where every flavour and texture comes together to create something entirely new and wonderful.[13] That's our world today—it's a multiverse where different realities, cultures, and ways of life don't just exist side by side; they intersect and blend in the most incredible ways. (The dessert, by the way, is halo-halo!)

---

13   *Anthony Bourdain: Parts Unknown*, season 7, episode 2, "Manila, Philippines,"
     presented by Anthony Bourdain, aired April 24, 2016, on CNN.

I remember when this really clicked for me. I was sitting in a meeting with my team at AVCommunications (AVC), looking around the room. We spoke twelve languages among the team members. That's when I realized the Multicultural Mindset I'd been developing isn't just about understanding different cultures—it's actually your personal GPS for navigating this borderless world.

Think about your own day. Maybe you start your morning with a traditional family breakfast, jump into a global Zoom meeting where you're connecting with colleagues across three continents, grab lunch at that new fusion restaurant downtown, and end your day watching a K-drama that somehow perfectly captures your own life experiences, even though you're not Korean.

This isn't just about being multicultural—it's about thriving in a world where multiple realities exist all at once. And just like I needed a GPS the first time I drove through Toronto's winding streets, we all need a navigation system to help us move through these intersecting cultural spaces. That's what the Multicultural Mindset is really all about.

You know what's beautiful about this? Once you start seeing the world this way, you realize that every interaction, every experience, every challenge is an opportunity to expand your understanding of this incredible multiverse we're all part of. And trust me, as someone who's gone from feeling like an outsider in her own cultural community to building bridges across countless cultural intersections, I can tell you that developing this mindset isn't just good for business (though it definitely is!)—it's transformative on a personal level too.

The Multicultural Mindset Framework

The Multicultural Mindset encompasses two critical elements: an acute awareness of rapidly evolving cultural dynamics in our interconnected world and the capacity to navigate, empathize with, and relate to cultures beyond our own experience. Developing a Multicultural Mindset begins with a fundamental yet challenging step: embracing humility. Accept that your worldview represents just one perspective among many, neither superior nor definitive. Sounds simple—but you'd be surprised what a difficult lesson it can be to learn.

Everyone begins their cultural journey within their own sphere of experience—this is both natural and universal. The Multicultural

Mindset framework guides you in expanding your knowledge and cultural fluency by increasing interaction and immersion in cultures beyond your familiar territory.

Building a Multicultural Mindset begins with intentional engagement with cultural spheres beyond your own. As your world expands, your cultural fluency and ability to navigate the Multicultural Multiverse naturally develop. Like peeling an onion, developing a Multicultural Mindset involves progressively deeper layers of understanding.

LAYER 1

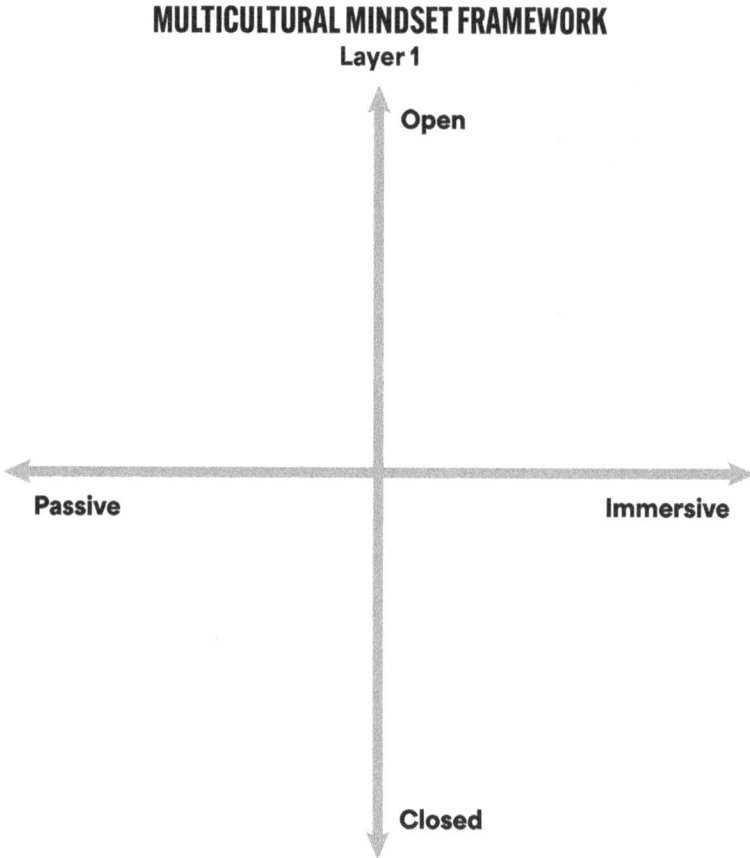

MULTICULTURAL MINDSET FRAMEWORK
Layer 1

Open

Passive

Immersive

Closed

The framework's foundation rests on two critical axes. The vertical axis measures mental receptivity—whether you demonstrate openness to cultural differences or maintain rigid boundaries. The horizontal axis measures engagement with cultural diversity—encompassing daily interactions across all social spheres.

In today's connected world, there are boundless opportunities for cross-cultural connections with people and communities outside your own language or background. From workplace relationships to community engagement, these interactions range from passive observation to active cultural immersion—which is the foundation for increasing your Multicultural Mindset and Quotient score.

LAYER 2

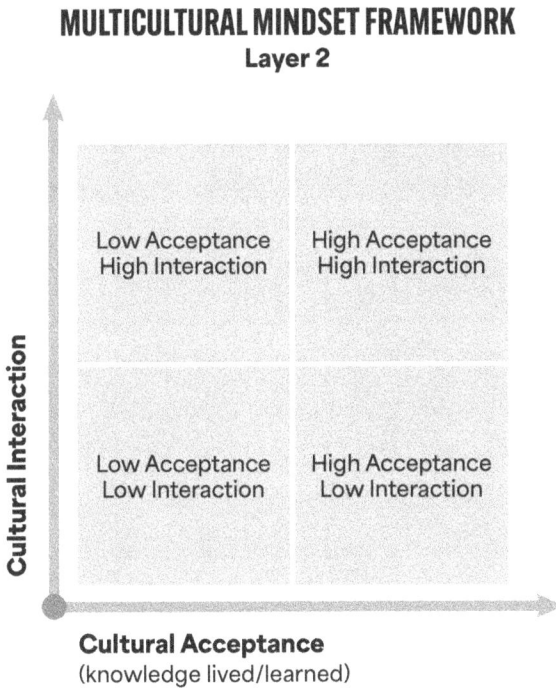

MULTICULTURAL MINDSET FRAMEWORK
Layer 2

Low Acceptance
High Interaction

High Acceptance
High Interaction

Low Acceptance
Low Interaction

High Acceptance
Low Interaction

Cultural Interaction

Cultural Acceptance
(knowledge lived/learned)

The second layer transforms openness into measurable cultural interaction: high cultural interaction or low cultural interaction on the vertical axis and high acceptance or low acceptance on the horizontal axis.

These axes evaluate both comprehension and receptiveness to cultural differences. You may demonstrate high understanding and tolerance while maintaining low interaction, particularly if your daily life primarily involves people within your cultural sphere.

I believe most people, myself included, start in the bottom left quadrant: low acceptance, low interaction. We all start in our own little sphere of influence or culture and that of our own immediate family. But over time, as you encounter more people outside your sphere, you move up the interaction axis. At the beginning of my journey, I was definitely in that quadrant. I lived in a Filipino household, eating Filipino food, with Filipino friends. I didn't have a lot of interaction outside of that bubble until I went out into the world and started interacting with more people.

Generally, as people increase their interaction with spheres outside their own, their level of cultural acceptance and MQ generally increases as well.

LAYER 3

MULTICULTURAL MINDSET FRAMEWORK
Layer 3

Knowledge

Online Exposure
Social Feed

Lived
Worked
Studied
in Another
Country

Travel &
in Real Life

Interaction Immersion

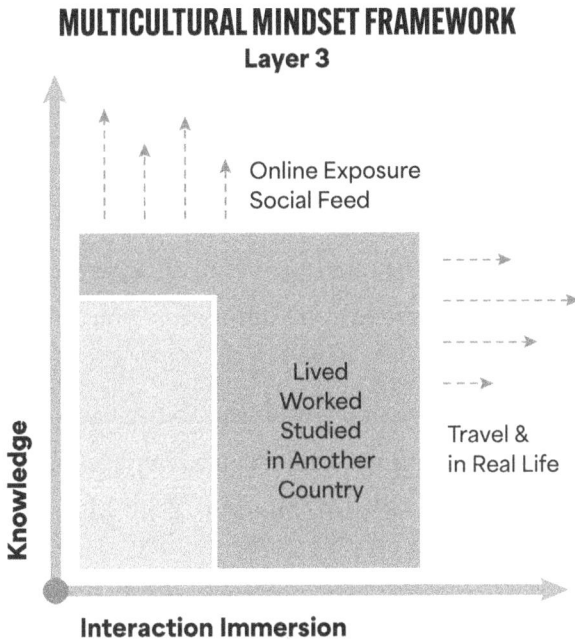

The third layer distinguishes between intellectual understanding and lived experience. While cultural knowledge can be acquired through media, literature, and digital content, nothing equals the depth of firsthand cultural immersion. You can watch a beautiful video of the Maldives, but that's not the same as immersing all your human senses.

Culture manifests through lived experiences. Travel offers unique opportunities for cultural exposure and understanding. However, meaningful cultural immersion requires intentional engagement beyond surface-level tourism.

The more you experience other cultures, especially through travelling, working, or living in other countries, or through immersing yourself, in real life, in other cultures that exist within your own country or city, your cultural understanding becomes broader and more expansive. You may have read many books, watched documentaries, or followed informative accounts on social media, which will give you a great deal of knowledge, but if you've never actually experienced another culture in real life, if you've never actually ventured outside of your own bubble, your position on the interaction and immersion axis won't change.

It is not inherently bad to exist in any of the quadrants in any of the layers of the framework. As we've discussed, that is where we all start out! But by moving toward openness and immersion, interaction and acceptance, and interaction and immersion, you can truly develop a Multicultural Mindset.

In our rapidly globalizing world, the ability to navigate cultural differences has become more than just an advantage—it's a necessity!

But how do we measure this mindset? With MQ.

THE MULTICULTURAL QUOTIENT

A Multicultural Mindset is the goal; the MQ is the tool to help you on your journey.

Think of the Multicultural Mindset framework as a map—the complete landscape of cultural competency with its various elements and interconnections. Your MQ then becomes your GPS system, providing specific coordinates of where you stand within this territory and suggesting potential routes for advancement. Together, they form a comprehensive system for both understanding and developing cultural competency in our modern world.

The Three Dimensions of MQ

Through my work with global organizations and diverse teams, I've identified three core dimensions that make up a person's MQ:

AWARENESS (THE FOUNDATION)

This is like learning a new language—you start with the basics in the culture wheel of knowledge: rituals, traditions, and beliefs. It's about understanding cultural patterns, recognizing different worldviews, and acknowledging your own cultural biases. I saw this in action when our team first started celebrating different cultural holidays— something I'll talk about more later in this book. The simple act of learning why Lunar New Year or Ramadan matter to our colleagues opened up new levels of understanding.

ADAPTATION (THE BRIDGE)

This dimension measures how effectively you can adjust your behaviour and communication style across cultural contexts. It's not about changing who you are but about expanding your cultural repertoire.

APPLICATION (THE IMPACT)

This is where the rubber meets the road—how effectively can you put your cultural understanding into practice? Can you lead diverse teams, manage cross-cultural projects, or innovate across cultural boundaries?

Ready to find out what your MQ is? Scan this link to test your own MQ.

Your MQ Score Explained

MQ evaluates your current level and capacity to understand, adapt to, and effectively operate across diverse cultural contexts. This concept builds upon the established frameworks of cultural intelligence created by Hofstede and Meyer while introducing new dimensions rooted in years of multicultural consumer research and demographic studies of our modern, interconnected society.

MULTICULTURAL QUOTIENT
(MQ)

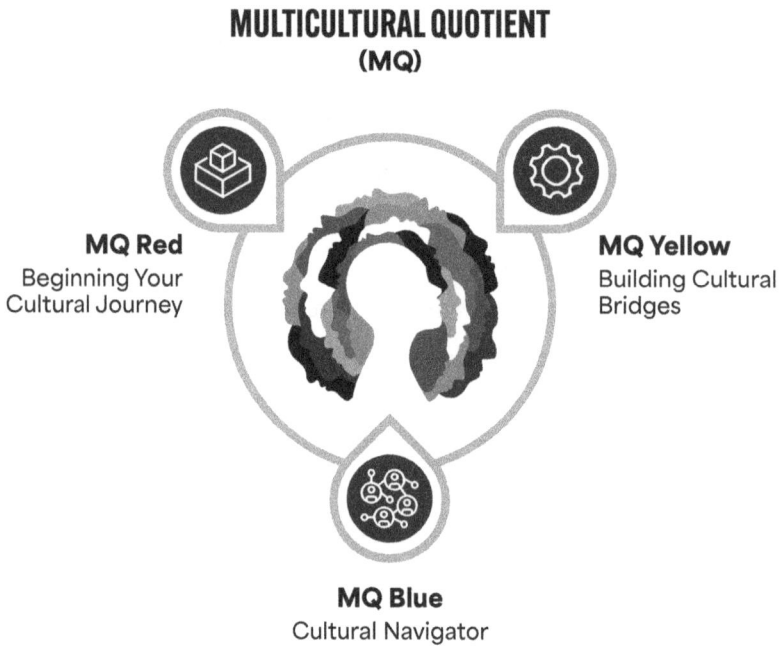

MQ Red
Beginning Your
Cultural Journey

MQ Yellow
Building Cultural
Bridges

MQ Blue
Cultural Navigator

RED
Multicultural Quotient (MQ)

MQ Red: Beginning Your Cultural Journey

Think of MQ Red as the starting line of an exciting journey. You're like someone who's just discovered a passion for cooking—you're learning the basics, getting familiar with the ingredients, and building your confidence. And that's exactly where everyone begins!

WHAT BEING AT RED MEANS:

- You're taking your first steps into understanding different cultures.

- You're developing awareness of cultural differences.

- You're building basic cross-cultural communication skills.

Why This Stage Is Important: You're laying the foundation for all future cultural learning. Just like learning to walk before you run, these first steps are crucial for your development.

YELLOW
Multicultural Quotient (MQ)

MQ Yellow: Building Cultural Bridges

Think of MQ Yellow as being like an adventurous traveller—you've got your bearings, you're comfortable exploring, and you're ready to dive deeper. You're like someone who's learned enough cooking basics to start experimenting with fusion recipes!

WHAT BEING AT YELLOW MEANS:

- You navigate cultural differences with growing confidence.

- You're developing a toolkit of cross-cultural skills.

- You're actively building meaningful connections across cultures.

Why This Stage Is Exciting: You're at a dynamic point where theory meets practice. You're not just learning about cultural differences—you're actively engaging with them.

BLUE
Multicultural Quotient (MQ)

MQ Blue: Cultural Navigator

Think of MQ Blue as being like a skilled cultural diplomat. You're like a master chef who can create beautiful fusion cuisines while respecting traditional recipes. You not only navigate different cultures with ease but also help others do the same.

WHAT BEING AT BLUE MEANS:

- You're a natural bridge-builder between cultures.

- You lead by example in multicultural environments.

- You inspire others in their cultural learning journey.

- You innovate in cross-cultural situations.

Why This Stage Is Transformative: You're not just participating in cultural exchange—you're actively shaping how different cultures interact and work together.

HOW TO BUILD A MULTICULTURAL MINDSET

We'll be spending the rest of the book digging into how you can go about cultivating your Multicultural Mindset using this framework—and there are also action steps and tips on the MQ site linked above—but here are some big-picture steps and actions you can take:

Increase your cultural awareness and immersion. Just as we talked about in the layers of the Multicultural Mindset framework section, awareness and immersion are the foundation for creating a Multicultural Mindset. This could include learning about different cultures by actively seeking out knowledge about their traditions, histories, and social norms—through reading or watching documentaries but also through real-world experiences such as travelling or engaging in cultural events.

Engage with diverse groups. In order to increase your cultural awareness and immersion, you have to get outside your own bubble. Intentionally seek out opportunities to interact with people who are outside your regular social or cultural circles.

Then, when you interact with those people, **practise active listening and empathy.** Listen to their perspectives. Walk in their shoes. And be open to what they say, think, and feel—even, or perhaps especially, if it is different from what you say, think, and feel!

This can help **develop your cross-cultural communication skills**—as can increasing your understanding of other cultures' social norms and communication styles, something we'll be talking about much more in chapter 7!

Along with developing your own Multicultural Mindset, **advocate for cultural inclusion** in your workplace, community, and social activities and circles. Support policies and initiatives that increase multiculturalism—and actively speak out and work against bias, inequity, and stereotyping.

Finally, remember that a Multicultural Mindset is an ongoing effort—so you need to **commit to lifelong learning and adaptation**. Commit to engaging with diverse groups in an ongoing way, not just as a one-off. As we've discussed, and as we'll come back to in chapter 8, the world is changing faster and faster thanks to technology. The world is not going to stop for you; to keep your Multicultural Mindset sharp, you need to keep learning, keep growing, and keep evolving!

All of these steps—and everything we will be talking about in the rest of the book—take time. In marketing, when you connect and then engage, you build a lifelong fan of your brand. Building a Multicultural Mindset is no different. First, you need to have the mindset of wanting to get out of your bubble; second, you need to seek a connection; and third, you need to engage on a deeper level. It has taken me my whole career to develop this mindset. You can't do it with the click of a button. You will not find this answer on ChatGPT—but you can find it through another human being, through their experiences, through their perspective.

WHY A MULTICULTURAL MINDSET?

As Michael Morris writes, the "us versus them" mentality that tribalism often fosters can lead to polarization, especially in politics and media, deepening ideological, cultural and social divisions—which in turn drives nationalistic movements and the breakdown of cooperation and mutual understanding.[14] In a nutshell, a Multicultural Mindset is needed not only for political spheres but also for everyday cultural interactions, influencing how people relate to their communities and the wider world.

---

14 Morris, *Tribal.*

And that wider world has so much to offer. You could just stay in your bubble, but if you do, you're missing out on the whole rich tapestry the world has to offer. I love all the cultures I get to experience that are not my own. They have enriched my life. I am better for knowing people who come from different backgrounds, faiths, and cultures.

Moreover, to understand yourself, you need to understand your place in the world—and our world is a Multicultural Multiverse. If you just stick your head in the sand and never look outside your bubble, you will never truly know yourself. Part of the slowing-down process is actually to consciously go inward first, not outward. Understand yourself, who you are, what spheres you exist in. Only then can you understand how you are connecting with and relating to those outside your sphere.

Getting out of your bubble does not mean erasing, ignoring, or forgetting your bubble. The Multicultural Multiverse is about celebrating your bubble, celebrating your culture, celebrating your identity.

And this includes every culture. Whiteness itself is a multiverse of cultures. Irish culture is not Italian culture is not German culture. The Multicultural Multiverse is not about skin colour; remember that in the culture wheel, skin colour is not even mentioned!

Rather than erasing individual cultures in favour of a homogenous, monocultural whole, the Multicultural Multiverse respects and preserves each individual culture.

We All Contain Multitudes

But the Multicultural Multiverse also goes beyond this, because it acknowledges and incorporates the fact that almost everyone will belong to more than one bubble in their life. The Multicultural Mindset framework actually challenges the idea that there are only two sides, only black and white—or red and blue. There's actually a rainbow—and the more colours you can see, the more complete your awareness and understanding of the world will be.

The Multicultural Mindset is more complicated and more diverse—and it's actually closer to the truth of what people really are. You will never be in one sphere, even if you started out in just one sphere. Hofstede mapped out the value systems of different cultures; but the fact is, while people may start in one culture, in one value system, based on where they were born and how they were raised, in this multicultural world, these values can shift and evolve.

Today, this is happening faster than ever—which we'll discuss in the next chapter, and which is the reason a Multicultural Mindset is not just a "nice to have"; it's a must-have. The Multicultural Era is already here—do you have the mindset to meet it?

KEY TAKEAWAYS

→ The Multicultural Mindset is made up of two key elements: awareness of the rapidly changing cultural dynamics of your world and the ability to navigate, empathize with, and relate to cultures outside your own sphere.

→ Building a Multicultural Mindset relies on intentional engagement with and immersion in cultural spheres beyond your own.

→ Your MQ is your GPS for navigating your journey through the Multicultural Mindset framework.

→ We are each our own Multicultural Multiverse, containing multitudes!

CHAPTER 3

WE ARE LIVING IN THE MULTICULTURAL ERA

"Multi-culture is the real culture of the
world—a pure race doesn't exist."

—Keanu Reeves

The question "Where are you from?" has followed me throughout my life. Born in Winnipeg, raised in Edmonton, and
now living in Toronto, my answer never seems to satisfy the
real question behind the surface question, "What is your
ethnic background?" Where we are from is still tied, in large part, to
ethnic origin. This is neither right nor wrong; it's just how things are.
This experience reflects a broader truth about identity in our modern
world—it's complex, layered, and often misunderstood.

Growing up, I was called many different derogatory terms for
various Asian ethnicities. It was deeply hurtful, though now I understand it was coming from a place of ignorance. Now I know that when
people asked where I was from, they were trying to place me within
their own context of understanding.

Today's reality shows how far we've come. When I say I'm Filipina, people understand the context and recognize the unique identity and culture this represents.

Today, access to the culture wheel is at an all-time high. Ethnic food stores and food options abound, and festivals celebrating traditions from many faiths and cultures are on the rise. Acceptance and representation are part of life today. The transformation is evident in our daily lives, and this shift represents more than surface-level change—it signals a fundamental transformation in how our society operates.

What has changed? The answer is simple: Multiculturalism has become mainstream.

MULTICULTURAL IS MAINSTREAM

Merriam-Webster defines "mainstream" as:

> *n. a prevailing current or direction of activity or influence*
>
> *adj. having, reflecting, or being compatible with the prevailing attitudes and values of a society or group* [15]

When something becomes mainstream, it transcends its original niche to become a prevailing current in society. With multiculturalism, we've reached this tipping point. While individual cultural communities might appear as distinct spheres, together they now form the dominant multicultural reality. In other words, when something becomes mainstream, it means it has become the norm—the dominant trend or way of thinking.

---

15   "Definition of MAINSTREAM," Merriam-Webster, accessed September 30, 2024, https://www.merriam-webster.com/dictionary/mainstream.

Now, this has always been true—even before the US and Canada were colonized, the indigenous peoples of these countries had multiple different cultures, not one homogenous culture. As these lands were colonized and became nations of immigrants, cultures from all over the world started to call the US and Canada home. At first, it was largely European cultures—English, Italian, Irish, Polish, Russian, all distinct cultures in and of themselves—as well as the cultures of the enslaved peoples brought to this land against their wills.

North American demographics are shifting toward a more diverse, urban, and globally connected population, with younger generations and recent immigrants driving these changes. This has implications for social interactions, cultural understanding, and the overall makeup of society in the coming years.

The transformation is particularly striking in Canada. According to Statistics Canada, "In the third quarter of 2024, international migration accounted for 92.0% of all growth," with 162,566 new permanent and temporary residents joining Canadian society.[16]

Looking ahead, projections paint an even more diverse portrait. By 2041, a record-high level of up to 34 percent of Canadians will be foreign-born—and a likely majority of the population, up to 52.4 percent, will be made up of immigrants and their children.[17] As of 2021, one in four Canadians had a mother tongue other than English or French,[18] while the 2021 Census documented "more

---

16   "The Daily—Canada's Population Estimates, Third Quarter 2024," Statistics Canada, December 17, 2024, https://www150.statcan.gc.ca/n1/daily-quotidien/241217/dq241217c-eng.htm.

17   Singer, "Immigrants and Their Children."

18   "The Daily—While English and French Are Still the Main Languages Spoken in Canada, the Country's Linguistic Diversity Continues to Grow," Statistics Canada, August 17, 2022, https://www150.statcan.gc.ca/n1/daily-quotidien/220817/dq220817a-eng.htm.

than 450 ethnic and cultural origins, 200 places of birth, 100 religions and 450 languages."[19]

The US mirrors this dramatic demographic shift and continues to inform the politics and policies. The Census Bureau reports that America's multicultural population has grown to 133.2 million, representing 40 percent of all Americans.[20] More significantly, Brookings Institution research shows that the under-eighteen population is now predominantly multicultural (52.7 percent), while interracial marriage has climbed to a historic high (11 percent).[21] And the Pew Research Center reports that future immigrants and their children will likely account for 88 percent of the US's population growth between 2015 and 2065.[22] Within Gen Z, 25 percent are Latino or Hispanic, 15 percent are Black, 6 percent are Asian or Pacific Islander, 5 percent are multiracial and 2 percent are American Indian or Alaska Native.[23]

This trend isn't isolated to North America—it reflects a global shift in economic power and consumer behaviour.

---

19   "The Canadian Census: A Rich Portrait of the Country's Religious and Ethnocultural Diversity," Statistics Canada, October 26, 2022, https://www150.statcan.gc.ca/n1/daily-quotidien/221026/dq221026b-eng.htm.

20   "National Population by Characteristics: 2020–2024," United States Census Bureau, December 2024, https://www.census.gov/data/tables/time-series/demo/popest/2020s-national-detail.html.

21   William H. Frey, "New 2020 Census Results Show Increased Diversity Countering Decade-Long Declines in America's White and Youth Populations," Brookings, August 13, 2021, https://www.brookings.edu/articles/new-2020-census-results-show-increased-diversity-countering-decade-long-declines-in-americas-white-and-youth-populations/.

22   Jeffrey S. Passel and D'Vera Cohn, "Immigration Projected to Drive Growth in US Working-Age Population Through at Least 2035," Pew Research Center, March 8, 2017, https://www.pewresearch.org/short-reads/2017/03/08/immigration-projected-to-drive-growth-in-u-s-working-age-population-through-at-least-2035/.

23   "What the Statistics Say About Generation Z," The Annie E. Casey Foundation, January 19, 2025, https://www.aecf.org/blog/generation-z-statistics.

THE GLOBAL ECONOMIC IMPACT OF MULTICULTURALISM

Global patterns reflect similar transformative shifts in multicultural economic influence. The landscape of consumer power is evolving across continents, driven by changing demographics and increased mobility. These demographic and economic shifts carry profound implications for global business.

According to the OECD's 2024 *International Migration Outlook*, 2023 showed record levels of migration flow, with 6.5 million new permanent immigrants throughout OECD members and partners, which encompasses thirty-eight countries around the world, including Canada and the US as well as the European Union.[24] This represents a 10 percent year-on-year increase and is 28 percent above 2019 levels.[25] In the European Union, 42.4 million people—9 percent of all EU inhabitants—were born outside the EU, and 11.2 million non-EU citizens were employed in the EU labour market.[26]

These demographic shifts carry profound implications for global business. As populations become more diverse, successful companies must adapt their strategies to serve increasingly multicultural markets. Understanding and responding to this diversity has become a crucial factor in business success across all major economies.

So here we are. We are living in the Multicultural Era, in which spheres of culture are colliding, interacting, and intersecting with each other. In this era, it is no longer practical—or even possible—to stay in your own cultural sphere, completely isolated from another sphere of influence.

---

24 "International Migration Outlook 2024," OECD, November 14, 2024, https://www.oecd.org/en/publications/international-migration-outlook-2024_50b0353e-en.html.

25 Ibid.

26 "Statistics on Migration to Europe," European Commission, November 5, 2024, https://commission.europa.eu/strategy-and-policy-priorities-2019-2024/promoting-our-european-way-life/statistics-migration-europe_en.

WHEN DID THE MULTICULTURAL ERA BEGIN?

The above statistics are modern-day measurements of the Multicultural Era, but some would argue that the Multicultural Era started millennia ago, as soon as different cultures started colliding. They might date the Multicultural Era back to the Silk Road, the ancient trade route that linked China to the West. This road carried people and ideas across great swaths of the world. Some might attribute the beginning of the Multicultural Era to colonialism, as the ruthless forces of colonial powers drove the movement and migration of populations around the world.

The rise of the modern industrial age and advancements in transportation further accelerated the speed of this cultural movement. We could fly across the ocean to visit a new country for the first time, no longer taking months to sail in a ship. This, I believe, was when multiculturalism started to become more mainstream, when the bubbles of culture in the world started to intersect more than they stayed separated.

If I were to name a start to the Multicultural Era, it would be 1973, when multiculturalism first became an official government policy. This happened to be in Canada, but it marked a new era for the whole globe. Canada was the first country in the world to officially make tolerance and acceptance of multiculturalism part of government policy. Since then, some other countries have adopted multiculturalism policies—and I hope even more will do so.

But today, another force is crashing the bubbles of culture into each other at a greater speed than ever before, making this era more multicultural than it has ever been before: the internet.

MOVING WITH THE SPEED OF CULTURE: CAN WE REALLY?

Culture moves as people move. One hundred years ago, migration was the driver. Forty years ago, the internet was the driver. In 2024, it's looking like AI will be the driver, assuming we continue to value speed over authentic connections.

In eras past, people had to physically migrate to experience new cultures. Culture moved when people moved, due to colonialism, trade routes, and emigration to different parts of the world because of unrest or war. Because of this, culture moved slowly.

Migration of people ➊ Awareness

The birth of the internet brought a massive reach of culture. People around the world could read and learn about places they had never visited, in ways they never could before. Culture started moving at the pace of the internet and 5G connectivity.

I am old enough to remember when the internet was born—I was in high school. By 1995, I was an early HTML web designer, helping "figure out" this new space called the internet. The effect of the internet on culture soon became a fascination of mine.

In college, my master's thesis was titled, "Marketing of Culture, Hybridity, and Identity in Virtual Spaces: A Virtual Ethnography of a Filipino-Canadian Circa 1998." As indicated by the title, I was writing this in the very early days of the internet. The internet was still in its nascency—so much so that my professors called my work "early online ethnographic research."

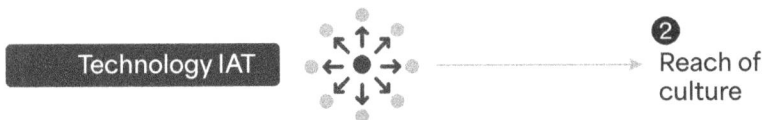

Technology IAT ➋ Reach of culture

Technology and the Internet of Things (IoT) created a new kind of community—a borderless one that could extend the reach of culture into more places. Online communities and fan groups were created. The number of people around the world who used the internet grew exponentially. Then came one of the most powerful forces of the modern era: social media.

SOCIAL MEDIA: DRIVER OF THE HIGH SPEED OF CULTURAL CONNECTIONS

Social media was born around 2000 and made it easier than ever to share and engage with cultures outside our own. Meanwhile, the speed of connection, driven by an algorithm unknown to human eyes, has slowly been curating our experience of the world.

Today, nearly five billion people in the world use social media— that's close to 60 percent of the world's population. The average person spends two and a half hours on social media per day—and this number doesn't appear to be decreasing with the variety and proliferation of platforms.[27]

Social media is an incredible tool, allowing people around the world to share and learn about cultures they might otherwise never encounter, exponentially increasing the exposure to and awareness of other cultures that define the Multicultural Era.

Social Media ⟶ ❸ Speed of connection

---

27   "Digital 2023 Global Overview Report: The Essential Guide to the World's Connected Behaviors," we are social/Meltwater, January 26, 2023, https://wearesocial.com/us/blog/2023/01/digital-2023/.

But there is also danger in culture moving at the speed of clicks. The faster the speed of information, the more quickly different cultures come into contact with each other—no matter where they are in the world. It's not just the reach of culture; it's the speed of it. All of these bubbles are not just oscillating; they're colliding faster and faster.

In his psychological and sociological studies, Michael Morris found that, in human nature, when the rate of change or new information is too fast, people revert back to a tribal state—a place of familiarity and comfort.

With the advent of the internet and social media, we are exponentially more exposed to the unknown and the sense of otherness outside our own worlds of knowledge. When we encounter things we don't understand, that are beyond our realm of knowledge, there is an animal instinct of fight or flight—with flight meaning retreating back to where you are comfortable. This in turn leads to social media often creating echo chambers that reinforce tribal identities, making it easier for people to isolate themselves from opposing views,[28] as Morris writes in *Tribal*.

Humans certainly have the capacity to learn, grow, and expand our knowledge—but when we are so inundated with infinite information at such high speeds, our rational, curious minds can't keep up with the rate of change. In other words, the speed of technology is too fast for the speed of culture. The speed of clicks is not the same as the rate of absorption. It is simply too much for the human brain to keep up with; we can't absorb it and make sense of it.

And even though these tools are purportedly meant to create connection, they can actually make it easy to disassociate and disconnect. We now rely on AI, on ChatGPT, to tell us everything. When we rely on technology for everything, we stop relying on other human

---

28   Ibid.

beings—we stop creating connection with each other and understanding each other on a deeper level. This leads to dissociation.

When everything is just a like or a swipe or a click, interactions become less meaningful. There is less opportunity to empathize, understand, or dive deep into the core of someone else's experience. You don't get down to the next layer of the mindset onion.

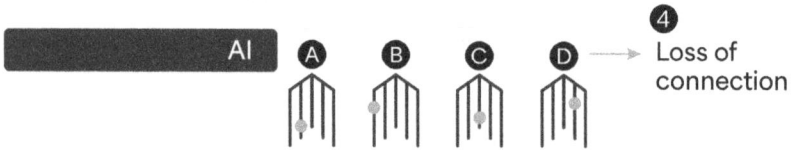

This is not to say meaningful human-to-human connections can't start through technology. Many meaningful relationships have started through a like on Instagram! But those relationships only became meaningful because they went beyond that one click or that one like and into a human interaction.

A Technology Paradox

AI is only as inclusive as we, the creators of it, are—something we'll talk about more in chapter 8.

While digital tools promise connection, they often create unexpected barriers to genuine cultural understanding. Our increasing dependence on AI and digital interfaces can inadvertently reduce human-to-human cultural exchange.

Digital interactions, while efficient, often lack the depth necessary for true cultural understanding. The complexity of cultural exchange cannot be reduced to clicks and likes—it requires genuine human connection. Digital tools provide information but cannot replace experiential learning.

Google or ChatGPT can help you increase your knowledge, but they don't increase your immersion. The internet—and increasingly

AI—are having an analogous effect to GPS. GPS is an incredibly helpful tool—and, as a result, many people now do not know how to read a map or how to find their way around without their phones. People get from one place to another by blindly following what their phones tell them to do, all while having no idea which way is north.

AI feeds the human tendency toward wanting instant gratification: Just tell me what I want to know right now. Why ask a human being, why engage in a whole conversation, if I can just get the answer from ChatGPT right now?

What does it mean when culture can come and go so quickly and superficially? There is a great need to rethink how we interact. This is why it is more important than ever to have a Multicultural Mindset front and centre. The baseline of the Multicultural Multiverse hasn't changed; what has changed is the speed at which it is moving and the way we need to navigate it.

This will remain true as technology continues to evolve—as we enter the age of AI. I believe AI will create loss of personal connection but greater opportunity for cultural nodes and currency to grow—something we'll talk more about in chapter 8.

But I don't think any of us really want a future in which we never interact with other human beings, only with technology. Interacting with human beings is the only true way to build understanding and connection. Yes, this takes more time—but slowing down and building real connection is the only way to reach true understanding and the only way to cultivate a Multicultural Mindset.

DRIVERS OF CULTURE

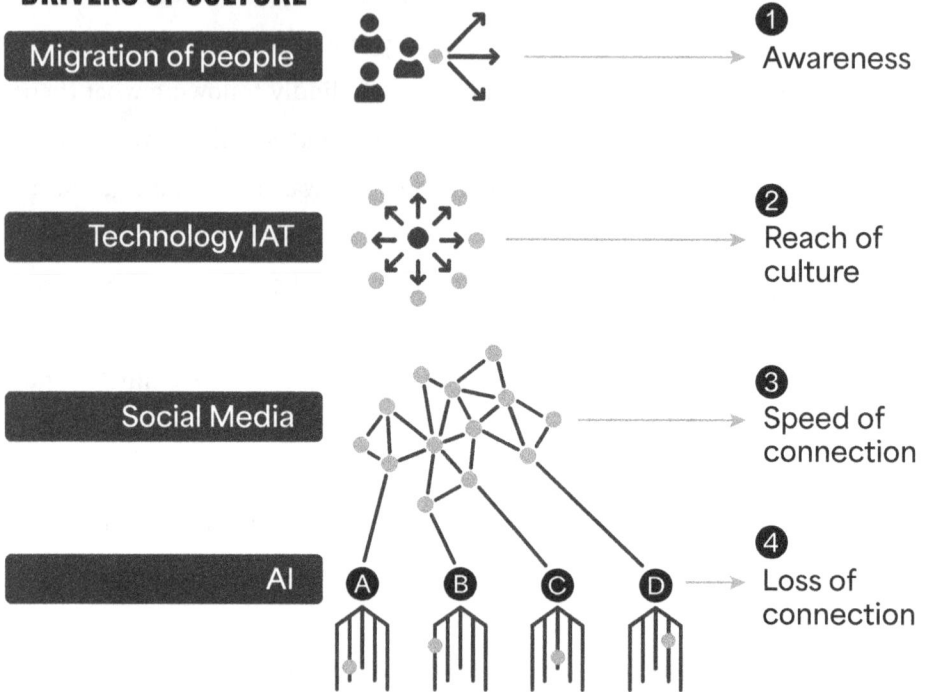

Migration of people		① Awareness
Technology IAT		② Reach of culture
Social Media		③ Speed of connection
AI	A B C D	④ Loss of connection

MULTICULTURALISM IRL

It isn't just virtual spaces that are contributing to the multiculturalism of the world. The real world—and individual people themselves—are becoming more multicultural.

There are already places in the world where the collision of cultures has created new cultures. I met a woman once who was Chinese Jamaican. She looked Chinese, but if you closed your eyes and listened to her, she spoke the most perfect Jamaican Patois! This struck me as a unique, almost jarring combination—but in fact, there are many Chinese Jamaicans because enslaved Chinese people were brought over to the Caribbean during the slave trade along with enslaved Africans, and they never left the islands. Now, the descendants of those enslaved peoples have created their own unique culture.

The fact is, people who have multiple cultural backgrounds or heritages are becoming increasingly common. According to the 2021 Census, 35.5 percent of Canadians reported more than one ethnic or cultural origin,[29] while in the US, more than 12 percent of the population now identify as "multiracial."[30]

Despite the growing prevalence of people with multicultural identities, there remains an obstinance against accepting this reality—as evidenced by US President Donald Trump's remarks in July 2024 about his opponent, Vice President Kamala Harris, who is a biracial American of both African and Indian descent.

At a conference of Black journalists, Trump stated of Harris, "She was Indian all the way, and then all of a sudden she made a turn and she became a Black person." Trump was seemingly unable to comprehend that a person could hail from more than one culture or ethnicity.[31]

Although this moment played out on a national (and even international) stage, it is far from the only instance of people not fully comprehending the reality of multicultural individuals. Multiple cultures existing within one person is something everyone in the world needs to become accustomed to—even people who inhabit so-called minority cultural spheres.

---

29 "The Canadian Census: A Rich Portrait of the Country's Religious and Ethnocultural Diversity," we are social/Meltwater, 2022.

30 Julie Bosman, Robert Gebeloff, and Ethan Singer, "Trump Remarks on Harris's Multiracial Identity Overlook a Growing Trend," New York Times, August 2, 2024, sec. US, https://www.nytimes.com/2024/08/01/us/trump-harris-black-asian-race.html.

31 Jonathan Weisman, Maya King, and Zolan Kanno-Youngs, "Trump Questions Harris's Racial Identity, Saying She Only 'Became a Black Person' Recently," New York Times, July 31, 2024, sec. US, https://www.nytimes.com/2024/07/31/us/politics/trump-kamala-harris-black-nabj.html.

The truth is, we *all* need to put in the work to readjust our mindset to the Multicultural Era. The good news is, the younger generations are, generally speaking, ahead of the curve and much more inclined toward a Multicultural Mindset. In a 2024 survey conducted by Ipsos and AVC, we found that, when asked about the amount of experience or interaction people had outside their own communities, Millennials and Gen Z had a higher experience quotient than older generations. This was true across all demographics—White, Asian, Latinx, South Asian, etc.[32]

Now, everyone else just needs to catch up—because these generations are the customers not just of tomorrow but of today. They are more globally connected, more accepting of world culture—and more inherently multicultural within themselves. If you cannot connect authentically with their sense of self and identity, you are going to miss out on a generation of customers who buy differently. The younger generations will break up with brands if they don't see them as authentic to their experience or supporting the causes they care about.

For example, in the 2024 Ipsos and AVC study, Gen Z and first-generation Canadians have distinct perspectives on diversity, are more likely to engage with media produced in countries outside of North America, and are most likely to say they feel close to people all over the world. Moreover, second-generation Canadians are most likely to say they have close relationships with people from various cultures—

---

32   "Defining Multiculturalism in Today's Canada," AVCommunications, September 2024.

meaning that the children of these Canadians may grow up with closer relationships as well.[33, 34]

THE EFFECT OF POLICY

The shift into the Multicultural Era, into multiculturalism being mainstream, may feel like it happened overnight. But it's the classic analogy of the frog in the pot of water. If you heat the water slowly, the frog doesn't notice—until all of a sudden, it finds itself in boiling water. This is what has happened with multiculturalism; it has grown slowly, and people haven't really taken notice—until all of a sudden, it is the norm.

This has resulted in an increased level of fear, especially in older generations, who in Canada, according to the Ipsos and AVC study, are more likely to live in rural areas, identify as White, and have little to no interaction with those of other cultures.[35] The fear of no longer being dominant, no longer being mainstream, is the fear of losing power that has powered political movements such as Brexit. People voted for Brexit from a place of fear, and the effects of that decision are still being felt today as they continue to shape policy in the UK.[36] Change is scary—and change is happening faster than ever, so fear is increasing faster than ever. We'll talk more about this fear factor—and how to overcome it—in chapter 7.

---

33 Ibid.

34 "Canadian, and Then Some: Landmark Study Maps the Multicultural Reality of Canadian Identity. 84% of Canadians Are Comfortable Expressing Their Cultural Identity While Still Feeling Canadian," Ipsos, December 12, 2024, https://www.ipsos.com/en-ca/landmark-study-maps-multicultural-reality-of-canadian-identity.

35 "Defining Multiculturalism," AVCommunications.

36 Pete Wilton, "Xenophobia Strongly Linked to Brexit Vote, Study Finds," Goldsmiths, University of London, November 29, 2017, https://www.gold.ac.uk/news/xenophobia-brexit/.

To a certain extent, embracing multiculturalism can happen on a national level, as it has in Canada. But even when a country doesn't have an official policy, it will still react to the Multicultural Era in some way.

People are proud of Canada *because* of its multiculturalism, not despite it. Seventy-seven percent of respondents felt that multiculturalism is an important part of Canadian identity; 75 percent felt having a diverse population is a very good thing for the country; and 69 percent felt multiculturalism strengthens the social fabric of Canada.[37]

Gen Z and second-generation Canadians are most likely to have close relationships with people from various cultures, while first-generation Canadians are more likely to say they interact or work with those different from them but mostly in passing. Third-generation+ Canadians are most likely to have limited or no interactions.

Which of the following best describes your interactions with people from other ethnic/cultural groups?

---

37   "Defining Multiculturalism," AVCommunications.

	GENERATION			
	GEN Z (n=230)	**MILLENNIALS** (n=563)	**GEN X** (n=427)	**BOOMERS+** (n=575)
have close relationships with people from various cultures/ ethnicities	**48%**	37%	37%	29%
work/interact with people from other cultures/ethnicities regularly, but mostly in passing or casual settings	35%	**45%**	**39%**	29%
have limited interactions with people from cultures/ethnici- ties different than my own	13%	13%	16%	**31%**
rarely, if ever, interact with people from other cultures/ ethnicities	4%	5%	9%	**11%**

	GENERATION IN CANADA		
	FIRST (n=485)	**SECOND** (n=360)	**THIRD+** (n=950)
have close relationships with people from various cultures/ ethnicities	37%	**46%**	31%
work/interact with people from other cultures/ethnicities regularly, but mostly in passing or casual settings	**44%**	32%	35%
have limited interactions with people from cultures/ethnici- ties different than my own	15%	18%	**23%**
rarely, if ever, interact with people from other cultures/ ethnicities	4%	5%	**11%**

"Defining Multiculturalism in Today's Canada," AVCommunications,
September 2024.

Because of its policies, Canada is cited by the Multicultural Policy Index as having one of the highest Immigrant Multiculturalism Policy Scores in the world—with the US scoring far lower on the scale.

COUNTRY	IMMIGRANT MULTICULTURALISM POLICY SCORE (OUT OF 8)
Australia ★	8
Austria	1.5
Belgium ★	5.5
Canada ★	7
Denmark	1
Finland ★	7
France	1.5
Germany	3
Greece	2.5
Ireland	4.5
Italy	1.5
Japan	0
Netherlands	1
New Zealand	6.5
Norway	4.5
Portugal	3.5
Spain	3
Sweden ★	7
Switzerland	1
United Kingdom	6
United States	3.5

"Immigrant Multiculturalism Policy Score," Multiculturalism Policy Index, accessed May 29, 2022, http://www.queensu.ca/mcp/.

But there doesn't need to be government policy to bring multiculturalism to life in any country, anywhere in the world. All it takes is a shift in mindset—a shift to a Multicultural Mindset.

THE MULTICULTURAL ERA IS HERE TO STAY

AVC's unofficial motto is "Multiculturalism is mainstream." We say it to each other here, around the office—and we have the stats to back it up, thanks to the Ipsos and AVC study. For example, 65 percent of Canada's population is multicultural.[38] These multicultural segments include

- temporary residents (nonpermanent residents with working VISAs and refugees),

- newcomers (one to five years in Canada, including permanent residents and international students),

- first-generation immigrants (five or more years in Canada), and

- second-generation Canadians (born in Canada to immigrant parents).[39]

The stats don't lie—and neither do the life experiences I, and I imagine you, too, have encountered in recent years. For example, twenty or thirty years ago, I was often the only woman and only minority in the room. Today, that almost never happens. Traditions such as Mardi Gras, St. Patrick's Day, and Easter were all European Christian holidays that have become widely celebrated.

---

38 "Topics, 2021 Census: Ethnocultural and Religious Diversity," Statistics Canada, December 4, 2024, https://www12.statcan.gc.ca/census-recensement/2021/rt-td/ethno-religion-eng.cfm.

39 "Defining Multiculturalism," AVCommunications.

Today, festivals and holidays such as Lunar New Year, Rosh Hashanah (the Jewish New Year), and Diwali (the Hindu festival of lights) are becoming much more widely acknowledged and recognized. I believe that within the next twenty years, these holidays will become as widely known and celebrated as European Christian holidays.

The Multicultural Era is here to stay—and embracing a Multicultural Mindset to meet this era offers more benefits than you can imagine.

KEY TAKEAWAYS

→ Statistics show that the world is increasingly multicultural—to the point where multiculturalism has truly become mainstream.

→ Social media and the advent of AI have increased the speed of cultural connections and intersections while also threatening to undermine authentic human connection.

→ Younger generations—the consumers of tomorrow—are more globally connected and accepting of world culture.

→ Policy does make a difference, as Canada's multiculturalism policy has proven.

CHAPTER 4

THE BENEFITS OF MULTICULTURALISM

"Uniformity is neither desirable nor possible in a country the size of Canada ... What could be more absurd than the concept of an 'all-Canadian' boy or girl? A society which emphasizes uniformity is one which creates intolerance and hate."

–Pierre Elliott Trudeau, Remarks at the Ukrainian-Canadian Congress, October 9, 1971

*I*n 2019, the Canadian branch of H&M, the international fashion retailer, hired AVC to create a campaign to establish a deep relationship with the most attractive and highest ethnic spenders in Canada: Chinese Canadians.

Many Chinese Canadians coming from mainland China, despite having moved to a new country, continue to use social media platforms from back home, such as Weibo and WeChat. This close-knit community regularly follows influencers on these platforms, who also impact their purchasing decisions. We knew that an app such as WeChat—the super app of mainland China—was the best way to reach this segment. However, there was a hitch: This would only cater to mainland Chinese and would potentially alienate Chinese people born in Hong Kong, Taiwan, and Canada, who cannot read the Simplified Chinese writing style.

So, we proposed an idea to H&M: Create an owned social media platform for the brand on WeChat—and make it bilingual.

We thought we might have an uphill battle getting this campaign approved. After all, WeChat was not as popular a platform in Canada as, say, Instagram. However, the general manager who approved this campaign, while originally from a Scandinavian country, had lived and worked in China. Because of that global experience, he understood the importance of WeChat.

So, when his marketing team said, "We need to invest to reach two million shoppers in Canada, and we want to use WeChat," he immediately understood it was the right thing to do. If he hadn't had that global knowledge, it probably would have been more of an uphill battle to get the campaign approved.

Our challenge was this: How do we get the target audience to follow a brand-new H&M WeChat Official Account *and* grow followers from scratch?

To accomplish this, we

- created a yearlong, always-on, bilingual content plan for the brand's first-ever owned WeChat account;

- drove engagement through contest promotions and through fashion and beauty influencers in Toronto and Vancouver, representing the mainland, Hong Kong, and Taiwanese segments;

- hosted a launch event the influencers could invite their followers to attend;

- leveraged other social media channels, such as Weibo, to attract new followers; and

- regularly partnered with different influencers to push H&M's content on the WeChat Official Account and engage with the audience.

The campaign was a raging success. It achieved the highest number of followers for a new WeChat Official Account in its first year in Canada.

This is just one example—and don't worry, I'll share more!—of how a multicultural marketing campaign can achieve spectacular results. The fact is, a Multicultural Mindset is beneficial across the board.

CREATING CONNECTION WITH CUSTOMERS

When I first meet with companies, one of the things they need to decide is why they should work with us instead of another agency that doesn't focus on multicultural marketing. They want to know, if they choose to commit to the Multicultural Mindset, how will they benefit? The answer is: in every way.

When I talk to my clients about why they need to invest in multicultural marketing, I tell them it is because a consumer is not just a consumer. A consumer is somebody who has an identity they're proud of, and they will act on that identity. This doesn't happen with regular consumerism; but if you can tap into someone's cultural identity, they will fight for what they feel is part of themselves. If you are not tapping into that, it is a huge missed opportunity. You will miss out on tapping into new consumers and audiences.

Multicultural businesses allow you and your brand to tell stories that tap into your customers' emotions. You can speak authentically to specific cultural groups because you have members of that group within your organization. You can respect and understand the nuances that make up these cultures, which allows you to create campaigns that are compelling. The more personal your marketing is, the more your customers will want your product, no matter what it is. It's one of those first tenets of marketing: Make it personal.

One of the first ways you can create this personal connection is through language. I often say to my clients, "You need to speak to your customers in their language of comfort—which may not be English." Not all companies or brands realize that the language of their customers' comfort may not be the one the leadership team speaks.

Go anywhere in the United States and you'll find Spanish-speaking frontline staff. Why? Because Spanish is the second-most spoken language in the US after English, and the US has the second largest Spanish-speaking population in the world[40]—and, therefore, having Spanish-speaking frontline staff helps with customer service. It helps make Spanish-speaking customers feel more comfortable, which improves their experience and makes it more likely the sale will be completed.

You don't have to be fluent in another language; just putting in the effort of saying "Hola!" instead of "Hello!" will be appreciated. Putting in the effort to learn to say hello or goodbye or thank you in someone else's language shows respect and attention.

There are two hundred languages spoken in the city of Toronto.[41] According to the 2021 census, 42.5 percent of Toronto residents have a mother tongue other than English or French, and 44.9 percent speak

---

40   Sonia Thompson, "The US Has the Second-Largest Population of Spanish Speakers—How to Equip Your Brand to Serve Them," *Forbes*, December 10, 2021, https://www.forbes.com/sites/soniathompson/2021/05/27/the-us-has-the-second-largest-population-of-spanish-speakers-how-to-equip-your-brand-to-serve-them/.

41   "Statistics on Official Languages in Canada," Government of Canada, August 14, 2024, https://www.canada.ca/en/canadian-heritage/services/official-languages-bilingualism/publications/statistics.html.

a language other than English or French (or in addition to English and French) at home.[42]

If you are a brand trying to reach new customers, how can you better connect? By finding ways to communicate in people's language of comfort. This doesn't mean they don't speak any English; they may speak English fluently. You are simply demonstrating a cultural awareness and understanding beyond your own point of view.

Language is a major driver of culture, and in today's world, multilingual skills are also an asset for employers. In the world of marketing and customer service, offering in-language allows brands to better connect with audiences. Why wouldn't you want to connect with a potential customer by saying hello to them in their language of comfort? It's a simple touch, but it makes a huge difference. It automatically establishes a level of comfort with your brand.

Back in the 2000s, I worked on an international campaign for Western Union called the "Yes Campaign." The idea behind the campaign was that Western Union moves money, and money makes the world go round, allowing for opportunities to impact change. When you move money with Western Union, you help pay for a kid's tuition, you help pay for a relative's medical care, you send your mom a Mother's Day gift, you help empower someone's life.

The narrative of the campaign was, "Can I make a difference in someone's life?" and the answer is, "Yes, with Western Union."

"Yes" is a very common word, but it is said differently all around the world—so this global campaign, which ran in twenty or thirty different countries—featured beautiful images of senders and receivers with the word "yes" in the language of the country in which the ad

---

42 "2021 Census: Language," City of Toronto, August 19, 2022, https://www.toronto.ca/wp-content/uploads/2022/12/93bb-2021-Census-Backgrounder-Education-Labour-Commuting-Language-of-Work.pdf.

ran. "Can I show love on Mother's Day, even though I'm a thousand miles away?" the ads asked. "Yes." Imagine that in Spanish, in Tagalog, in Punjabi, in Mandarin.

This was the first time a global brand had truly embraced multilingualism within one ad campaign. Up until then, big global companies would just write an ad in English and call it a day, figuring people know how to speak at least some English in every country around the world. But when you put the word *sí* in front of people in Mexico, people feel like the brand is speaking specifically to them. They feel seen and understood.

Western Union remains one of AVC's best clients—and the "Yes Campaign" isn't the only successful multicultural campaign we've run for them!

CASE STUDY

Western Union's Boonununus Campaign

In creating a new campaign for the Jamaican diaspora in the US, we leveraged the cultural insight around the importance of expression, song, and dance rooted in everyday life. After three rounds of brainstorming, our creative team, which included a diverse team of designers, writers, and strategists, including some from Jamaica, landed on a nostalgic but relevant word in Patios: Boonununus.

Go ahead, Google it!

This vernacular word, pronounced "boo-nuh-hun-nuss," means a bonus of happiness. We decided to centre the campaign around this idea—positioning sending money home via Western Union as the ultimate expression of love.

We wanted to create an ecosystem of happy moments for the audience, weaving in the music and dancing that is so integral to Jamaican culture.

To keep the treatment authentic and rooted in Jamaican culture, the agency launched a mega-celebrity collaboration for the brand with DJ Drama and Mr. Vegas, two renowned names that instantly increased brand love. The musical video collaboration featured a soundtrack that became a hit single and captured the streets of Philly at its vibrant best, instantly resonating with the audience. The film brought alive the true essence of Boonununus.

Boonununus made waves across social media, digital banners, POS, influencer marketing, and TV. We're talking $0 meals at Jamaican restaurants during the campaign period, offering a unique experience to customers while creating awareness about the offer.

We also roped in popular Jamaican influencers who spread the Boonununus love in their own unique styles across Instagram and TikTok. They seamlessly spread the message of sending money home to loved ones, something very close to the hearts of all Jamaicans in Philadelphia.

What started as an idea soon took shape as an integrated campaign, and the numbers are proof! The campaign garnered millions of impressions, and the film reached well over a million views on social media—which led to thousands of conversions and hundreds of app downloads.

This campaign was truly multicultural. We spoke the language of the brand and the community. We captured the essence of Jamaican culture. And we successfully delivered the brand message.

The result? Boonununus!

DRIVING ENGAGEMENT THROUGH MULTICULTURAL MARKETING

Multicultural marketing is vital—and yet many brands aren't willing to put sufficient resources toward it. I once worked with a fast-moving consumer brand that told me it was very committed to multicultural marketing—but this billion-dollar company was investing less than $100,000 a year in it.

© marketoonist.com

Most brands will invest around 10 percent of their annual budget in multicultural marketing initiatives. To put that into perspective, if they spend $100 on marketing, only $10 of that is spent on multicultural marketing. But far more than 10 percent of the population is multicultural. Wouldn't it make sense to have the percentage of the budget allocated to multicultural marketing match the percentage of your market that is multicultural?

For example, in Toronto, half the population is multicultural[43]—meaning they are born somewhere else, they immigrated or are the children of immigrants, they speak another language, etc. If your market is Toronto, why would you not allocate 50 percent of your budget to multicultural marketing to reach that 50 percent of the population?

If you don't invest in multicultural marketing—and if you don't pay attention to the multicultural world around you—you will miss out on engagement-building opportunities.

Five years ago, we were working with a client who was trying to reach South Asian customers, a diverse multicultural audience covering different languages, faiths, and unique cultures. One tradition that united them? Cricket. According to World Sports, it's the number one sport for nearly one billion people on the planet!

Cricket is a highly watched sport in many markets, with a huge following in South Asia, but it had not yet caught on in North America. Our advice to this brand was to get in on the ground floor. There were title sponsorship opportunities, partner opportunities, so many ways it could take advantage of the global popularity of cricket. But the brand declined to take action.

A few years later, the International Cricket Competition descended on North America, featuring a full-page ad in *The New York Times*—which has since become very famous—depicting the Statue of Liberty holding a cricket bat. "Cricket has arrived," the ad proclaimed.

The South Asian community could not have been prouder—and I can guarantee that brands that got in on the ground floor of cricket

---

43 "2021 Census: Citizenship, Immigration, Ethnic Origin, Visible Minority Groups (Race), Mobility, Migration, Religion," City of Toronto, November 4, 2022, https://www.toronto.ca/wp-content/uploads/2023/03/8ff2-2021-Census-Backgrounder-Immigration-Ethnoracial-Mobility-Migration-Religion-FINAL1.1-corrected.pdf.

sponsorships and partnerships saw the benefit. Meanwhile, the brand we worked with came to us and said, "Now, we would like a strategy around cricket." If it had taken our advice five years ago, it would have reaped the benefits of being first to market. Now, it had missed its moment.

When consumers see brands supporting the things that are important to them—such as the sports they love from their country of origin—it creates a sense of connection and understanding. The community feels seen and validated. In order to do this, you have to keep your ear to the ground. Culture happens at the grassroots level. If you are tapped into the Multicultural Multiverse, you can be ahead of the game.

In Canada, Canadians have noticed an increase in diversity in advertising, yet many view it as inauthentic or trend driven. Younger generations, particularly first-generation Canadians and Gen Z, are especially critical of this lack of authenticity, but they are also the most inclined to trust brands that demonstrate a genuine commitment to diversity and inclusion.[44]

Multicultural audiences are the future of global commerce. Businesses and brands that understand this, that pay attention early, are the ones that will get that first mover advantage and reap the benefits. Otherwise, they will be like that company that only got onto the cricket bandwagon *after* there was a full-page ad in *The New York Times*.

Applying cultural sensitivity to your wider business strategy will ensure that you can effectively market the right products in new segments, leverage your brand against foreign competitors and foster brand loyalty with local customers. As you do this, you need to also make sure you are being sensitive and paying close attention. You don't want to put your foot in your mouth when trying to land the

---

44   Ibid.

right message because that can actually hurt your brand. The devil is in the details, as they say, so make sure you're paying attention to the little things along the way.

If you don't, you might end up like the Tesco in London that put up a Ramadan display offering bacon-flavoured Pringles—observant Muslims, such as those who would be observing Ramadan, strictly don't eat pork! The display sparked much outrage (and amusement) from the Muslim community, and Tesco apologized and removed the display.[45]

More recently, actor Simu Liu called out a company selling its version of boba tea. In an episode of *Dragon's Den* (the Canadian equivalent of the US's *Shark Tank*), a pair of Quebec entrepreneurs were seeking funding for their bubble tea brand, Bobba, which they claimed had "transformed" boba tea.

Liu immediately pushed back. "There's also an issue with cultural appropriation," he said. "There's an issue of taking something that's very distinctly Asian in its identity and 'making it better,' which I have an issue with." He continued, "I'm studying your can and I am looking for anything that tells me where boba came from, and where boba came from is Taiwan. Not only do I feel like this is not happening here but that I would be uplifting a business that is profiting off of something that feels so dear to my cultural heritage. I want to be a part of bringing boba to the masses, but not like this."[46]

While half of the Dragons (including Liu) passed on investing, three were still interested, and one, Manjit Minhas, agreed to invest in

---

45   Doug Bolton, "A Tesco Used Bacon-Flavour Pringles in a Ramadan Promotion," *The Independent*, June 24, 2015, https://www.the-independent.com/news/weird-news/a-london-tesco-used-smokey-baconflavoured-pringles-in-a-ramadan-promotion-10343223.html.

46   Sabrina Weiss, "Simu Liu Accuses Boba Brand of 'Culture Appropriation' in Viral Dragons' Den Clip—Then $1M Investment Is Pulled," *People*, October 17, 2024, https://people.com/simu-liu-accuses-boba-brand-of-culture-appropriation-in-viral-clip-dragons-den-8730049.

the product. But that wasn't the end of it. After the segment aired, Liu's response went viral—and social media was firmly on Liu's side. The pressure was so great that Minhas decided to withdraw her investment.

Bobba eventually posted an apology on its Instagram page, vowing to reevaluate to "reflect a respectful and accurate representation of our Taiwanese partnership and bubble tea's cultural roots." But the fact is, all of this could have been avoided if the company had simply had the appropriate people at the table and involved in the conversation from the beginning. As Liu said in the segment, "What respect is being paid to this very Asian drink that has blown up around the world? Is it in your teas? Is it in your product development? Who is on your staff? Who is on your cap table that is providing that for you?"[47]

In 2024, Heinz had to pull two of its ads (by two different agencies) after they were called out for insensitive racial tropes—one for imagery reminiscent of minstrel shows and one that featured an interracial couple getting married but omitted the Black father of the bride, inadvertently reinforcing the stereotype of absent Black fathers.[48]

If you have a diversity of perspectives and backgrounds at the table, you have some checks and balances in place. If there had been a Muslim person at the table when Tesco was planning its display, it never would have made it into stores. If there had been an Asian person at the table when Bobba was creating its product, it would probably have secured that investment. If there had been Black voices in the room at those two advertising agencies, they would have created different ads for Heinz.

---

47   Ibid.

48   Hannah Bowler, "Brands Let the DE&I Fire Burn Out. Can the Heinz Controversy Reignite It?" *The Drum*, October 15, 2024, https://www.thedrum.com/news/2024/10/15/brands-let-the-dei-fire-burn-out-can-the-heinz-controversy-reignite-it.

CASE STUDY

What Happens Without Multicultural-Minded Leadership

A major technology company engaged my company to create a Lunar New Year campaign featuring a major Chinese celebrity. It was the first time the brand had invested in the market; now, it cited the huge opportunity to tap into 1.4 million potential new customers as its reason.

The marketing leaders who were advocating for the campaign were strong allies to the Chinese community from the beginning. They understood the value of the potential market and came in with the intent to include the community at every stage of the campaign. They also identified that their competition was already in the space, and something needed to be done to gain share of voice. They built the business case and, brief in hand, committed a six-figure budget to the effort.

How did this company get a foothold here, when so many brands were still struggling to get executive support? Simple. The marketing leaders were themselves members of the Chinese community—one Chinese American and one Chinese Canadian. They knew the value of the campaign. They knew what the celebrity meant to the community, and they could see how it would help drive the brand. The goal was to create a connection—and it built engagement even beyond what we expected. Sales grew. Customer engagement grew. ROI was in hand for this one campaign. I thought we were on the path to building multicultural marketing innovation globally.

Then, the company restructured, and people were let go—including these two marketing leaders. Almost immediately, the business case and momentum died. Why? Because nobody was advocating for multicultural marketing at that brand anymore. It was one and done.

Without a multicultural champion to raise their voice, the ROI, the budget, or the passion for representation, campaigns unfortunately come and go. This is why the Multicultural Mindset must be embedded throughout the organization, not just resting with one or two people—and it has to start with leadership.

BENEFITS ACROSS YOUR BUSINESS

We've been talking a lot about the importance of multiculturalism in marketing—marketing is, after all, my background! But the benefits of a Multicultural Mindset in business extend far beyond marketing. A Multicultural Mindset can apply to every aspect of business—from how you interact with customers to how you hire and work with employees. A Multicultural Mindset can help train frontline staff to better work and serve the communities in which your business operates. A Multicultural Mindset can help attract—and retain—a diverse and devoted workforce.

Diversity is good for business. If you had a hockey team, would you only want defensive players? No—you would of course want good offensive players who bring different skill sets and perspectives. The more diverse your workforce, the wider the variety of skills and perspectives you have access to.

In my business, I consciously make the decision to hire people who are not like me. I also, of course, look for people who are right for the job—but I am looking for diversity. When I took over AVC five years ago, there was not a lot of diversity. I think there were only two languages spoken across the entire team.

Now, we have twelve languages spoken across the team. Members of our team have lived and worked in at least ten different countries. Over this same span of time, our business grew fourfold. Employee retention went from 90 percent turnover to 90 percent retention—a 180-degree turnaround. Client satisfaction scores went from 50 percent Net Promoter Score (NPS) to over 90 percent NPS. Client loyalty and new client acquisition grew more than threefold. While there were multiple factors driving the growth of the business, I can confidently say that hiring people who were not like me, who had different backgrounds and skill sets and perspectives, had a huge impact.

LEVERAGING MULTICULTURAL LEADERSHIP

The benefits of a diverse workforce are myriad—but only if you leverage that diversity. Large organizations are often inherently diverse because of their sheer size—but they don't leverage the benefits of that diversity, of the knowledge and understanding they already have within the company.

In October 2024, I had the pleasure to interview Joy Chen of the Multicultural Leadership Institute. Drawing on her experience as a former deputy mayor of Los Angeles and a Fortune 500 executive recruiter, Chen emphasizes the importance of cultural agility and the ability to navigate diverse business environments as critical components of modern leadership.

In my interview with Joy, she shared a heartfelt story about how her father avoided attending a party that reflects on her family's immigrant experience and cultural assimilation. The story underscores the complexities her family faced as Chinese immigrants navigating American society, where cultural norms and expectations were often unfamiliar. Her father, an MIT-educated immigrant, wanted to fit in, but the experience emphasized the challenges of bridging two worlds—of balancing his traditional Chinese roots with the new American cultural environment. This anecdote is part of Joy Chen's broader narrative about the immigrant journey and how it shaped her perspectives on leadership and inclusion. It serves as a metaphor for the struggles many immigrants face in integrating into a new society while maintaining their cultural identity.

In November 2024, I sat down with the marketing director for Diageo Canada, Nadia Niccoli, to talk about leadership in multicultural Canada. Nadia shared with me that over 50 percent of the leadership positions in Diageo are held by women and/or people of colour.

Diageo was formed in 1997 with the merger of Grand Metropolitan and the Irish brand Guinness. From its roots, Diageo has grown into a global organization focused on creating an inclusive and empowering organizational culture. Leadership that values local market structures and ensures that diverse voices are heard plays a crucial role in guiding the organization toward better decision-making. This type of leadership goes beyond policies; it is about setting a tone of inclusion and trust, which empowers employees to be their authentic selves, whether through neurodiversity initiatives or support for health and well-being, as seen in programs such as those available in Canada.

My conversation with Nadia demonstrated to me how valuing emotional, financial, and personal well-being allows leaders to create a culture of trust in which individuals feel empowered to contribute their perspectives. Ultimately, multicultural leadership is about building a sense of community and collaboration, encouraging leaders to take risks, embrace challenges, and connect with their teams on a human level. This leads to better decisions, a stronger sense of belonging, and a commitment to reconciliation and collective progress.

MEET MR. FOX

How can you build up multicultural leadership skills? It starts with valuing multicultural experience. One of my first mentors was an Irish Canadian man named Brian Fox. He was the executive who brought me into a global enterprise. He hired me because of my marketing experience and geographic location—but my Multicultural Mindset and experience gave me a competitive edge in the hiring process. I represented one of the company's largest customer bases globally. And Brian knew that having cultural insight would be critical for the job ahead. We also connected on a shared passion for music and numbers.

Up to this point in my career, I had worked at professional service firms and nonprofits in Canada, and this was my first time interviewing at a global company. I was greatly surprised when half of my interview focused on my community and volunteer work—which, at that time, was 100 percent within the Filipino community. I was the youth editor for the Filipino newspaper. I volunteered with a Filipino organization that helped new immigrants settle and bridge the language barrier when they moved to Canada. They asked me if I spoke Tagalog.

I walked away from that interview wondering why they were so focused on my volunteer work. Why did they care so much about my background and experience with these Filipino organizations? I had always downplayed my multilingualism and multiculturalism in my career. Now, that's exactly what the hiring manager was interested in! Brian knew it could lead directly to more insights about a customer base he didn't understand, about whom nobody on the team had in-depth knowledge.

Brian taught me a lot about the importance of building diverse teams and practising a Multicultural Mindset. He would attend every cultural event. He knew greetings in every language spoken in the office. He actively sought to learn more about the customers and teams he was leading. He was intentional about being inclusive and seeking diverse and sometimes divergent perspectives to bring to the table. And while he didn't always get it right, he was always open to continuous feedback.

When the time came for my promotion to lead the Canadian marketing and product team, I was grateful to have a mentor like Brian who, like me, was also learning to navigate the nuances of culture and business in a global enterprise.

VALUING GLOBAL EXPERIENCE

Recent studies from the Conference Board of Canada reveal a startling statistic: Skill shortages accounted for 7 percent of the productivity gaps during the two most recent periods in which Canadian productivity lagged behind that of the US. Without those shortages, Canadian GDP would be up to $26 billion larger.[49] And yet, as the Surepoint Group reports, "Canada has a large pool of highly skilled immigrants, many of whom are not able to work in their chosen fields due to a lack of recognition for their foreign credentials."[50] Indeed,

---

49   "Skills and Productivity: Which Skills Shortages Are Impacting Canadian Productivity?" The Conference Board of Canada, August 15, 2024, https://fsc-ccf.ca/wp-content/uploads/2024/08/skills-shortages-impacting-productivity_aug2024.pdf.

50   "The Labour Crunch: Why Is There a Skilled Trades Shortage in Canada?" EnergyNow.ca, May 17, 2023, https://energynow.ca/2023/05/the-labour-crunch-why-is-there-a-skilled-trades-shortage-in-canada/.

"Success in addressing skills imbalances through immigration requires not only that programs target in-demand skills and understand the transferability of skills between occupations, but also that these skills and qualifications of new Canadians are recognized and accepted by employers," the Conference Board of Canada states in its report.[51] This disconnect stems from an outdated perception: the mythical requirement for "Canadian experience."

The paradox in the American job market is similar: 70 percent of employers say they are having a hard time finding talent, with only seventy-one workers for every one hundred jobs[52]—and yet the US is failing to attract and employ global talent.[53] This disconnect persists despite clear evidence that global perspective brings tangible value to organizations.

The evidence is compelling; global experience translates directly to business success. McKinsey's 2023 "Diversity Matters Even More" report demonstrated that companies in the top quartile when it came to executive team diversity had a 39 percent greater likelihood of financial outperformance versus their bottom-quartile peers.[54] A BCG study of 1,700 companies in eight countries found that companies with above-average diversity in their leadership teams reported 19 percent higher innovation revenue than companies with below-

---

51 "Skills and Productivity," The Conference Board of Canada.

52 Tracy Bower, "Yes, the Talent Shortage Is Real: What You Must Know to Attract and Retain," *Forbes*, February 12, 2024, https://www.forbes.com/sites/tracybrower/2024/02/12/yes-the-talent-shortage-is-real-what-you-must-know-to-attract-and-retain/.

53 Karen Aho, "America Is Falling Behind in the Global Talent Competition," *Immigration Impact* (blog), July 26, 2023, https://immigrationimpact.com/2023/07/26/america-falling-behind-global-talent-competition/.

54 "Why Diversity Matters Even More: The Case for Holistic Impact," McKinsey & Company, December 5, 2023, https://www.mckinsey.com/featured-insights/diversity-and-inclusion/diversity-matters-even-more-the-case-for-holistic-impact.

average diversity.[55] Companies that prioritize diversity also have 5.4 times higher retention rates and score higher on customer satisfaction, employee engagement and development, and financial strength.[56]

So, let's flip the narrative. Instead of asking "Do you have Canadian experience?" or "Do you have local experience?" we should be asking "What global insights can you bring to our organization?" or "How has your international experience shaped your problem-solving abilities?" or, my personal favourite, "What cultural perspectives will you add to our team?"

International experience creates new spheres of culture in which multicultural experiences enhance ability to navigate different contexts. The more nodes you develop, the stronger your MQ and cultural fluency become. Think of it as compound interest for your career currency.

My own experience illustrates this perfectly. What landed me the job wasn't just my marketing skills—it was my ability to understand and navigate multiple cultural contexts. In fact, 56 percent of employers expect their demand for bilingual and multilingual speakers to skyrocket in coming years.[57]

55   Rocío Lorenzo et al., "Diverse Leadership Teams."

56   Tory Clarke, "Three Reasons the Case for Corporate DEI Programs Is Stronger than Ever," *Forbes*, November 28, 2023, https://www.forbes.com/councils/forbeshumanresourcescouncil/2023/11/28/three-reasons-the-case-for-corporate-dei-programs-is-stronger-than-ever/.

57   Rachel Wells, "Multilingual Speakers Wanted: Job Demand Surges for the Next 5 Years," *Forbes*, October 16, 2023, https://www.forbes.com/sites/rachelwells/2023/10/16/multilingual-speakers-wanted-job-demand-surges-for-the-next-5-years/.

GOING DEEPER

Global experience isn't just a "nice-to-have" credential anymore—it's becoming a critical driver of business performance. As organizations navigate increasingly complex international markets, teams with diverse global perspectives are delivering measurable advantages across multiple business dimensions. The data tells a compelling story: Companies that effectively integrate and leverage global talent are seeing significant improvements in key performance indicators.

A Multicultural Mindset gives you a competitive edge and benefits every aspect of your business. But you have to do more than check a box or meet a requirement. You have to really embrace it. The businesses and brands that really embrace the Multicultural Mindset are the ones that will see the biggest benefits.

People care about authenticity—especially the younger generations, who are the future of the market and the workforce. In fact, 74 percent of Gen Z respondents in the Ipsos and AVC study agreed that brands have a responsibility to promote multiculturalism.[58] To attract the next generation, you need to demonstrate an understanding that is deeper than surface level—as we'll talk about in the next chapter.

As we move deeper into the Multicultural Era, the ability to navigate multiple cultural contexts isn't just an advantage—it's a necessity. Organizations that recognize and leverage global experience will lead the next wave of innovation and growth.

---

58   "Defining Multiculturalism," AVCommunications.

KEY TAKEAWAYS

→ A Multicultural Mindset allows you to tap into multicultural markets in a more authentic way, creating deeper connections and stronger engagement with customers.

→ Having multicultural leadership prevents embarrassing cultural missteps.

→ Studies show that valuing global experience and diversity leads to tangible business benefits across the board, from greater innovation to higher revenue.

CHAPTER 5

MORE THAN SKIN DEEP

"If I'm an advocate for anything, it's to move. As far as you can, as much as you can. Across the ocean, or simply across the river. Walk in someone else's shoes or at least eat their food. It's a plus for everybody."

–Anthony Bourdain

Going deeper in the building of cultural fluency and mindset takes time and effort—but it doesn't have to be complicated or difficult. In fact, it can be as simple as asking "Why?" five times.

Several years ago, I hired an art director to work on a creative campaign for a major food retail brand. The major retail holiday season was Lunar New Year, a particularly important retail season, as millions of people in North America observe the festival. In the process of ideating a creative design for the campaign, the art director landed on showcasing a Chinese family eating dim sum around a well-appointed table.

"Why do you want to show a family enjoying dim sum?" I asked.

THE MULTICULTURAL MINDSET

"Well," the art director, who was Chinese himself, said, "it's what my family eats during Lunar New Year."

"That's great," I replied, "but can you explain the cultural insight behind the selections shown here? Why dumplings specifically?"

"Because they're round, they look like the moon, they're symbolic, they carry a lot of cultural meaning."

"Ah, I see. And the moon is important because … it's Lunar New Year?"

The conversation continued, and we eventually landed on the why: There were *no* other stock photos available that adequately showcased the tone, action, and images of a Chinese family celebrating Lunar New Year. When left with no options other than a stock photo of a family eating dumplings, he felt he had no other choice but to "go with it." The root of the decision was simply because the image was available—but it wasn't actually the best solution.

This scenario illustrates a broader challenge in today's digital marketplace: While 74 percent of consumers consider representation crucial in their brand engagement decisions,[59] marketers and content creators face a persistent shortage of authentic, culturally nuanced imagery. The traditional stock photo landscape remains surprisingly homogeneous, often falling into what is called "diversity theatre"— superficial representations that fail to capture the nuanced reality of different cultural experiences.[60]

After understanding the limitation of the stock photography available, we went back to the client to explain the challenge.

---

59 Sonia Thompson, "What Consumers Want You to Know About Representation in Marketing," Inclusive Marketing, 2021, https://inclusionandmarketing. com/2021-representation-in-marketing-study/.

60 Matt Shipman, "Study Underscores Lack of Diversity in Stock Photography Sites," *NC State News* (blog), February 1, 2023, https://news.ncsu.edu/2023/02/ diversity-photography-health-comms/.

We recommended another solution: to curate the right photo for the scene, with the right tone and the right balance—which required a custom shoot and a bigger budget. We added the explanation that while the stock photo showcasing a family eating dumplings was "technically OK," it could also be taken as stereotypical and blind to the nuances of a diverse Chinese culture that may consume other kinds of food.

In the end, the entire process of asking why and the resulting custom photo shoot took six more weeks of work and a major push to meet the timeline for the holiday season. But the client, and their customers, were better for it.

Job done. Right?

I wish it were that simple. But there's a follow-up question: Why is there such a limited inventory of diverse imagery for this major cultural celebration globally?

The answer reveals a systemic challenge: While specialized platforms such as Pocstock are working to address this void, popular searches of stock photo sites such as Shutterstock still reveal a startling lack of diversity.[61] Research shows that 67 percent of consumers report that seeing themselves authentically represented influences their purchasing decisions[62]—yet the available imagery often relies on tired stereotypes or feels artificially staged, missing the authentic moments that resonate with audiences.

Often, the root of cultural understanding can mean taking time and extra effort. And sometimes, the power of asking why can literally create a ruckus to clients' budgets. It challenges us to move beyond convenient solutions and push for authentic representation, even

61   Melvin Espinal, "The Stock Photo/Video Industry Has a Diversity Problem," iPullRank, July 30, 2020, https://ipullrank.com/the-stock-photo-video-industry-has-a-diversity-problem.

62   Thompson, "Representation in Marketing."

when it requires additional resources, time, and commitment. The stakes are simply too high to settle for anything less.

THE POWER OF WHY

Asking "Why?" five times has become standard practice at my marketing agency, AVC. Sure, it takes longer, but you get to a deeper understanding. Every time you ask "Why?" you peel back another layer of the onion. By taking the time to go to the deepest level, you're able to better connect with employees, colleagues, and potential customers.

We all speak from our own personal experience. If you ask five people the same question, you'll probably get five different answers based on each person's personal perspective. However, if you ask each person "Why?" five times, you'll get closer to a truth you may not have been able to see at the outset.

I started this practice in 2019, when I took over the company and was looking for a structured framework for my team to follow to avoid falling into stereotyping or bias—and we use it all the time. Consider this example: We were working with a company that wanted to reach newcomers in Canada. "Great," we said. "Why are newcomers in Canada an important segment for you?"

"Well, because we've heard there are a lot of people moving here from India and China, so we need to target those audiences."

"Why are you focused only on those two communities—Chinese and Indian?"

"Because we feel our budget can only extend to cover those two markets."

"Why would you not want to target all newcomers regardless of origin or language?"

And on we went, challenging the company at every step until it realized it needed to do more work to understand the mindset of newcomers rather than just thinking about race-based immigration data that made the company view these segments as homogenous.

Asking why becomes even more critical when addressing complex organizational challenges. At a conference I attended recently, I met a C-level executive who was being asked to scale back diversity, equity, and inclusion (DEI) initiatives in response to what they called "DEI fatigue."

"Why did they ask to scale back?" I asked.

"Because there has been pushback about these initiatives taking too much focus."

"Why do you think there is resistance now?"

"Because there is no one left to help champion it, I think. I'm the last one on the team."

"Why don't they hire additional qualified people to support you?"

"Because there are *no* other people of colour on the team—it's just me. And I'm tired, Joycelyn. I'm really trying but am just tired of being a one-person DEI initiative."

"Why don't we go get a drink?" I quickly suggested. "I'm here to listen and totally feel the same sometimes."

This small interaction revealed that "DEI fatigue" was also affecting those it was intended to help—and there were resourcing gaps affecting inclusion efforts.

Asking why helps get to the root understanding of most issues— and it also allows us to build more cultural fluency. In the first example, it led the client to check their own bias about newcomer communities. In the second, it revealed a real gap in the resourcing of DEI initiatives. Cultural bias or gaps in understanding happen all the time, especially when decisions are made in a cultural vacuum.

The five whys technique helps break out of that vacuum, to dig deeper to understand the fundamental human needs, aspirations, and potential that lie beneath and beyond the exterior.

BEYOND SKIN COLOUR AND LANGUAGE

For businesses seeking to attract new customers, business partners, or employees, it's easy to fall into a cycle of checking a box. DEI initiatives abound in corporations with the intent to create more representation in all aspects of an organizational culture.

"We are committed to representation," I've seen many brands say proudly on their websites or social media. "We translate all our marketing material into Spanish (in the US) or French (in Canada)," the brand will say, or proudly highlight, "Look! We did this ad last year and hired a multiracial cast." While this effort is noted and appreciated, this is usually where I push a little more.

"That's great," I will reply, "but translation alone and ethnic-focused casting is just the start. We need to go *beyond* skin colour and look deeper at the culture you wish to connect with."

Say, for example, you're from an island nation such as the Philippines. You probably won't see much multicultural marketing because the population is not particularly multicultural. If you then moved from the Philippines to the US or Canada, it would be jarring—all of a sudden, you are no longer in the majority but part of a Multicultural Multiverse. In the Philippines, all the marketing would be in Tagalog, your language of comfort. The people in the ads would look like you, and the places would look like places you know. It would all feel like home. If you relocate to Brooklyn, New York, that will no longer be the case—and you'll be looking for a hint of yourself, of something that reminds you of home. This is why in most cities, little enclaves of culture pop up—Little Manila, Little Puerto Rico, Little Jamaica, etc.—because people are looking for that connection and community that feels like home.

Now, if you are a brand, why wouldn't you lean into this? Why wouldn't you try to give that person a hint of home? Why wouldn't you say "Kamusta!" instead of "Hello"? As we discussed in the previous chapter, speaking to people in their language of comfort is an incredibly powerful form of connection. But this is just a starting point, a way to open the door. Don't stop there. You need to go deeper than just putting a phrase through Google Translate and slapping it onto an ad.

When a brand says to me, "We're going to save money and put our materials through Google Translate, what do you think?"—first, I say, "Forget what I think. Let's go ask the customers." Try putting an ad through Google Translate and putting it out there—see what customers say about it. See if they understand it. The majority of the time, something will be off—because language is nuanced, and AI translators, which are often not trained with diverse language or cultural nuance, are not there … yet. We'll talk about this more in chapter 8!

Second, you have to understand that multiculturalism also goes beyond language. After all, language is only one element in the culture wheel. All of the culture wheel elements are interrelated. Just because you put a line in Tagalog on your website, it doesn't mean you have actually taken the time to learn about Filipino culture or to get to know the Filipino community.

If you look back at the culture wheel, you'll also notice that one element is not included: ethnicity and race. Although that information shows up often in stats and data—White, Black, Hispanic, Other—and carries over into how we think, we need to think beyond those labels. Simply putting a person of colour in an advertisement doesn't constitute multicultural marketing. It doesn't create an authentic connection with a specific cultural community; all it shows is that you cast an actor or model with a certain skin colour. To reach customers, you have to tap into something more than just their skin colour.

Breaking markets down by skin colour or ethnicity also ignores the reality we discussed in chapter 3: We exist in a Multicultural Multiverse. When AVC was working with Ipsos on our 2024 study, the Ipsos team told us this study was ahead of its time in that it was redefining how people think about multicultural markets. Many brands think of multicultural marketing as talking to separate, distinct communities—separate, distinct spheres. But that does not reflect the actuality of the Multicultural Multiverse.

From back in the days of *Mad Men*, when Madison Avenue was the beating heart of the marketing industry, advertising was always guided and shaped by mostly middle-aged White men. A powerful but homogenous group of people would curate the industry's baseline and shape society's tastes. Today, culture is more democratized and diverse—and we all need to be able to connect in a relevant way with a more diverse population if you want to succeed.

Unfortunately, the industry still lags in shaping the voices from within. In 2021, 73 percent of agency CEOs, owners, and C-suite executives identified as White. This figure increased to 90 percent in 2023, indicating a regression in leadership diversity. Black representation among agency leaders fell from 5 percent to 0.75 percent, while Asian and Hispanic leaders decreased from 12 percent to 1.5 percent.[63]

---

63   Jameson Fleming, "In 2021, 73% of Agency Leaders Were White. In 2022, It Was 90%," *Adweek* (blog), August 8, 2023, https://www.adweek.com/agencies/in-2021-73-of-agency-leaders-were-white-in-2022-it-was-90/.

GET OFFLINE AND IMMERSE

When I say "relevant," you might immediately think of whatever the most recent TikTok trend is. And sure, you can tap into those trends—but going deeper requires going beyond just what you see online, as data points are just that: points in time.

In the world of multicultural marketing, brands and marketers are trying to do their best to represent a community and be authentic, but they're relying on tools such as Shutterstock or Getty Images or an AI that may not have been trained or stocked with culturally nuanced or vetted information (something we'll be talking about more in chapter 8).

Recalling Morris's *Tribal*, we know that human instincts for belonging, identity, and group dynamics shape modern interactions. Whether it's a live concert, a cultural festival, or an in-person team retreat, these moments tap into our innate need for collective identity. The sights, sounds, and energy of an in-real-life (IRL) group create tribal connections that are, per Morris, biological. And you just can't get that online—after all, I don't think anyone could claim that watching a video of Taylor Swift performing is the same as being at the Eras Tour in person, surrounded by fellow Swifties!

Unlike online interactions, which can be filtered or anonymized, IRL moments strip away pretence and encourage authenticity, deepening active versus passive relationships within the "tribe."

You can passively Google or ask ChatGPT and passively watch TikToks or follow accounts and like posts on Instagram—but that is just surface level. The ChatGPT shortcut is negating our ability to experience things that need time and literal physical human connection in order for them to truly imprint on our brains. To go deeper, you have to keep asking questions and seek out experiences—and, ideally, actually talk to the human beings who are part of that culture. That is immersion, as opposed to passivity.

I always tell my team: You're not going to get ahead in your career by talking to a room full of people who are just like you or by never leaving your house and just staying in your pajamas on Zoom. You need to go out into the world. I had one person on my team who would say, "Oh, we don't need to go meet the clients in person. We can just invite them to this virtual reality event." While that may be cool, it will never replace the connection made when you invest the time to meet somebody in person—just like reading about or watching a video of an event online will never replace the experience of attending that event live.

Morris reminds us that rituals performed IRL carry more weight. The physical act of gathering in a specific place for a shared purpose evokes a primal sense of belonging and commitment. The path to going deeper—as the Multicultural Mindset framework lays out—is through research, understanding, and immersion.

I once met a CMO for a major consumer products company. As a fellow judge in the Canadian Strategy & Marketing Awards, he shared his team's approach to IRL marketing immersion. On his team, desk research or googling something was not good enough! Instead, he sent his brand managers to live in a house with customers of the product in order to view, observe, and really "live" alongside the customer. They would observe the customers, ask them questions, and see how they used the products in practice. The market research wasn't passive; it was full-on immersion.

Now, I know this sounds extreme. Would you leave the comfort of online tools to spend two weeks away from home living among strangers for the pursuit of market research and customer insight? Most would not—but I always remember the lesson he shared around the jury table. Lazy marketing was pervasive in the industry. We had lost sight in the forest, with all those data points swirling around us. Why did we need immersion, when there was already so much data around us to draw from?

Why indeed? Ask it again—five times!

In my own experience, the most impactful lessons I learned about multicultural communities came through IRL experiences. For example, I attended my first Vaisakhi festival in Surrey, British Columbia, in 2007. Vaisakhi is the Sikh celebration of harvest and new year, celebrated by millions of people of the Sikh faith worldwide. In Canada, entire streets are shut down to allow for a beautiful parade of floats, music, and celebration. And yet somehow, despite living in Canada my entire life, I didn't experience a Vasiakhi event until I was thirty years old!

It only took thirty seconds, with the polite gesture and education of a friend and colleague, to teach me the rituals of the tradition that would stick with me forever. "You need to cover your head in the temple area, Joycelyn," Ranbir whispered. "You are totally welcome, just keep your head covered and follow my lead."

Ranbir's willingness to teach me about his community and the Vaisakhi festival opened my eyes to the beauty of a culture I did not understand at all. This one immersive experience, with a member of that community who welcomed me in and made me feel comfortable, allowed me to go further and deeper in my understanding of this culture. I tried the food, I sought out more information, I asked questions—and I made friends. Now, I have people in my circle from that community who I can say "Happy Vaisakhi!" to every year—and with some understanding of what that holiday means to that community.

Going deeper requires more time and effort. You can't just eat a samosa and say, "I understand Indian culture." You have to talk to people in that community and experience the culture firsthand—and be open to and respectful of that culture's traditions and behavioural and communication styles. The samosas I did, in fact, eat at the temple during that first Vaisakhi festival with Ranbir were even more meaningful, as I learned the samosas and food were often given to members of the community, and even outsiders, for free as an act of charity and community.

This kind of immersion is something you can encourage as a leader. At AVC, one of the practical things we have done to increase cultural awareness and immersion is to have cultural immersion days, where we as a team all celebrate holidays together, even if they are from cultures other than our own. Everyone learns about Rosh Hashanah. Everyone learns about Ramadan. Everyone learns about Lunar New Year. We serve the food associated with the holiday and learn about the practices and rituals. If this practice sounds familiar to you, it's probably because many schools have these kind of cultural immersion events or activities—and they are just as effective in the workplace.

GOING DEEPER: CULTURAL IMMERSION AT HOME AND ABROAD

Building your Multicultural Mindset requires more than just being present in a space—it's about genuine engagement and respect. Experiencing new places, spaces, and cultures is a gateway to developing your Multicultural Mindset. And travel could be across town for the purpose of sharing a simple meal—as Bourdain also noted, "Food is everything we are. It's an extension of nationalist feeling, ethnic feeling, your personal history, your province, your region, your tribe, your grandma. It's inseparable from those from the get-go."[64]

For example, during my first visit to Cuba, I stayed at a beautiful resort with amenities and great food. The staff were all Cuban, and the location was in a rural part of Cuba, away from the more commercialized urban city centre. But was I immersed in the Cuban culture vacationing with other Canadians, staying in the resort? Was I getting out of my cultural sphere of comfort? Of course not.

Yet sometimes, the most profound cultural discoveries happen not in crossing oceans but in crossing streets. In New York City, where over seven hundred languages echo through neighbourhood streets[65] and nearly 40 percent of residents were born in another country,[66] cultural immersion opportunities unfold daily across the five boroughs.

Take the growing Filipino community in Woodside, Queens, known affectionately as "Little Manila." Here, the scent of freshly baked pandesal wafts from traditional bakeries each morning, while modern Filipino fusion restaurants reimagine classic adobo and sinigang for new generations. It's where the Filipino value of "kapwa"—shared identity—comes alive through simple acts such as sharing a plate of lumpia with neighbours or joining the excited crowds at the annual Philippine Independence Day parade.

Cultural immersion through travel enhances your Multicultural Mindset in a number of ways. First, it fosters a global perspective by encouraging direct engagement with diverse cultures. For example,

64   Kathryn Schulz, "Eat Your Words: Anthony Bourdain on Being Wrong," Slate, May 31, 2010, https://slate.com/news-and-politics/2010/06/eat-your-words-anthony-bourdain-on-being-wrong.html.

65   "Languages of New York City Map," Languages of New York City, accessed February 1, 2025, https://languagemap.nyc/.

66   "2023 Annual Report on New York City's Immigrant Population and Initiatives of the Office," NYC Mayor's Office of Immigrant Affairs, 2023, https://www.nyc.gov/assets/immigrants/downloads/pdf/MOIA-Annual-Report-2023_Final.pdf.

cultural exchange programs have been shown to develop soft skills such as adaptability and problem-solving, contributing to increased cultural awareness and personal growth.[67]

A 2022 study found that 90 percent of travellers actively seek to experience destinations as locals do, while almost half are concerned their travel experiences are not culturally authentic, indicating a strong interest in meaningful cross-cultural interactions.[68] Travel remains a powerful tool for fostering empathy, tolerance, and a shared sense of humanity, with direct benefits for both travellers and host communities.

I didn't actually travel much as a kid. Vacations were expensive, so the extent of our family vacations were more akin to *National Lampoon*'s road-trips-gone-bad than anything resembling cultural immersion. At this point in my life, I was definitely MQ Red!

It wasn't until my professional career took off that I had the privilege to travel outside of North America. Within five years, I had become a lifetime gold member of a hotel chain for having spent 200 nights a year in a hotel. And while, yes, much of that time was spent in a meeting room or a taxi (akin to staying in the resort), with each adventure I became a little braver. I'd venture out from the hotel further and for longer periods. I was adding on extra vacation days post-trip to take time for personal travel. Working for a global company afforded me the opportunity to travel extensively and in turn build up my immersion experiences through travel. Slowly but surely, I moved from MQ Red to MQ Yellow.

---

67   Abbey Goers, "Report Finds Study Abroad Strengthens Soft Skills and Cultural Awareness, Improves Career Prospects," University of Wisconsin-Stout, November 25, 2020, https://www.uwstout.edu/about-us/news-center/report-finds-study-abroad-strengthens-soft-skills-and-cultural-awareness-improves-career-prospects.

68   Kayla Medina, "2023 Travel Trends: US Travelers Aim to Experience Destinations as Locals and Crave More Authenticity," Get Your Guide, November 15, 2022, https://www.getyourguide.press/blog/2023-travel-trends-u-s-travelers-aim-to-experience-destinations-as-locals-and-crave-more-authenticity.

Several times I travelled with colleagues and witnessed firsthand the challenge of working and travelling with little to no cultural immersive experience. During one such trip, I was in Asia on a market tour to countries such as Thailand, Vietnam, Hong Kong, and the Philippines, travelling with a number of my colleagues who had never travelled outside of their country of origin—and it was evident with some of these individuals that the effort of travel caused a great deal of anxiety about the unknown. They weren't comfortable leaving the hotel at night. They didn't want to try any of the local food offered by the local teams. Without any prior knowledge of or immersion in a culture, space, traditions, and rituals outside their own, the travellers felt like fish out of water.

On another business trip, I was with an entourage of government and business delegates on a market tour in the Philippines. Some major dignitaries were in town for the company-sponsored event, and senior staff from the company were invited as well. There was a star-studded entertainment list, like the Grammys of the Philippines, with a red-carpet gala feel for us, the company representatives. We flew twelve hours to attend this one event; it was a big deal! As we gathered in a fancy hotel ballroom, the program began on time with a formal address from the president and the acknowledgments of the visiting dignitaries. But one of the key dignitaries, a senior vice president, was nowhere to be found. Still asleep in his room? Jet lag perhaps? No one could get ahold of him.

Finally, he showed up—very late—and failed to recognize the lapse in formally greeting hosts of the event. Filipino business culture, like many in Southeast Asia, has more formality than traditionally seen in some other cultures. So, when the senior vice president stood up to leave the event less than one hour after arriving late, without any formal greeting or thank-you to the hosts, it did not go unnoticed.

Perhaps this individual was simply unaware of the behavioural norms of this culture—which is not his fault. Perhaps he was simply MQ Red. Whatever the reason, the lack of etiquette at this formal event was so shocking that I could hear the chatter among the tables with important business partners—partners with whom this event would have a lasting impact on future business dealings and meetings.

This experience highlighted for me the importance of cultural awareness—and of being aware of what you don't know when immersing yourself in a culture outside your own sphere. If this executive was simply acting from a place of not knowing, a Multicultural Mindset might have led him to do some research into the behavioural norms of the country he was visiting—or to ask respectful questions about the culture and behavioural expectations once he had arrived.

I carried this lesson with me as I encountered cultures I was unfamiliar with later in my career. For example, a few years later, I was invited to represent my company at a community event being hosted by leaders of the Nigerian Igbo community in Alberta, Canada. When I arrived, I was told to prepare for the "kola" presentation.

In Nigerian business culture, the kola nut ceremony symbolizes hospitality, respect, and the fostering of relationships. Offering and sharing kola nuts, alongside prayers for prosperity and unity, is a traditional way to welcome guests, establish goodwill, and build trust, underscoring the importance of mutual respect and collaboration. It is a deeply meaningful gesture during business meetings, negotiations, and partnerships, and embracing this tradition can help strengthen ties and demonstrate cultural sensitivity.

Now, in all honesty, I did *not* know any of this at the time. I was scared—I didn't know what I was walking into. But my Multicultural Mindset gave me assurance that I could keep an open mind and respectfully ask questions to determine the appropriate way to act.

The ceremony involved the tribal chiefs from the Igbo community—all men—presenting me with a kola nut. I wasn't sure what to do with it; I didn't know what to do or what to say, and I didn't want to mess up because I was representing the company. I felt like a fish out of water. All I could do was try to be as open and respectful as possible in this totally unfamiliar situation. So I said thank you and was very appreciative.

The event was supposed to start at six in the evening and end by nine. Unfortunately for me, I did not understand the unwritten rules of time in the community. The event actually started at nine (so I ended up missing my flight back home), and I found myself sitting around for three hours. But I knew I couldn't leave as the senior vice president had done earlier in the Philippines; I needed to be respectful of this important cultural event, regardless of whether I completely understood it. I was deeply thankful for the cultural immersion I had experienced so far in my life that had allowed me to develop my Multicultural Mindset and reach MQ Blue!

Upon learning of the importance of the kola nut presentation, which I was able to do in those three hours I was waiting and chatting with the community, I knew I had to more deeply express my gratitude, so I expressed my thanks on stage and later wrote a heartfelt note of thanks. I understood they had given me this honour as the representative of a brand that was supporting their community. Often, African cultures are lumped together into one Pan-African mass, all represented the same way—when in fact, there are myriad unique cultures.

Whether travelling abroad or exploring diverse communities at home, the key is meaningful engagement. When I encountered the kola nut ceremony with the Nigerian Igbo community in Alberta, I approached it with the same openness I bring to exploring Jackson Heights, where Indian spices and Tibetan momos mingle with

Colombian arepas, or Sunset Park, Brooklyn, where Chinese seniors practise tai chi above streets humming with Latin American rhythms.

Most communities simply want to be seen and acknowledged. Whether it's respecting the formality of Filipino business culture during that eventful meeting in Manila or understanding the significance of timing in the Igbo community celebration in Calgary, cultural fluency develops through genuine interaction and respect. It's not about going outward; it's about going deeper—whether that journey takes you across oceans or just across town.

The world isn't just at our doorstep—it's our home. And as my experiences both abroad and in local communities have taught me, developing a Multicultural Mindset isn't about the distance travelled but about the depth of engagement and understanding we're willing to pursue.

STRENGTH IN THE MULTI AND THE MANY

Developing genuine cultural fluency and mindset requires more than cursory exposure—it demands systematic engagement with multiple perspectives and deep immersion in diverse communities. A common misconception in organizations is the reliance on a single cultural representative—the notion that one individual can serve as a spokesperson for an entire ethnic or cultural group. This oversimplification undermines the complex tapestry of experiences that exist within any cultural community.

The reality is that no single Indian, Chinese, or Filipino voice (yes, even mine!) can adequately represent the perspectives of millions. While individual relationships—whether with colleagues, friends, or community members—provide valuable starting points for cultural understanding, they should serve as gateways to broader engagement rather than endpoints in themselves.

This depth of cultural understanding requires substantial investment: rigorous research, comprehensive analysis, and sustained engagement with diverse communities. Organizations often benefit from partnering with cultural expertise—whether through multicultural marketing agencies, cultural consultants, or diversity specialists—that can facilitate deeper understanding and more nuanced approaches to cross-cultural engagement.

While data and analytics play a crucial role in this process, authentic cultural understanding transcends mere statistics. Contemporary marketing has perhaps overcorrected toward pure performance metrics at the expense of human insight. The most effective marketers embody multiple disciplines; they are part data scientist, part psychologist, part artist, and part anthropologist. Relying solely on data analytics while remaining detached from direct cultural engagement leaves three-quarters of the marketing equation unexplored.

This understanding led to the development of AVC's comprehensive model for cultural engagement. We call it the AVCs:

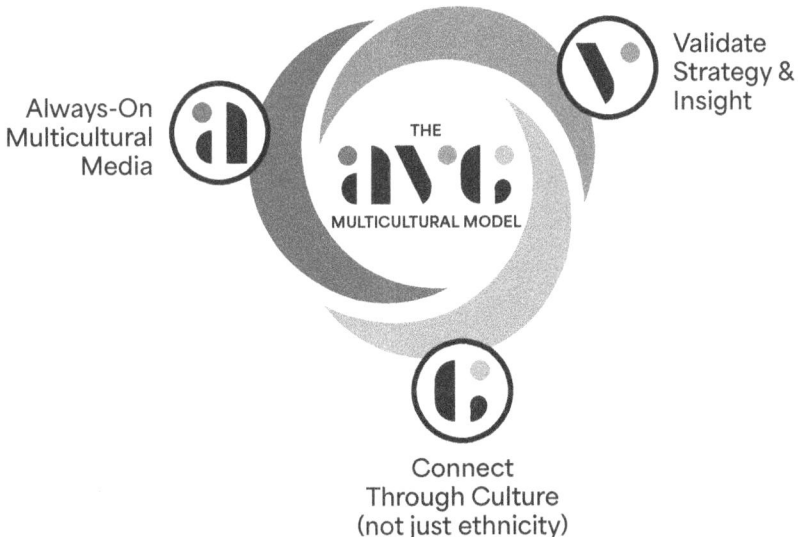

THE
aVC
MULTICULTURAL MODEL

Always-On
Multicultural
Media

Validate
Strategy &
Insight

Connect
Through Culture
(not just ethnicity)

A is for Always On. You need to be thinking about this all the time. For some brands, the extent of their multicultural marketing is one seasonal campaign for one week out of the year. But culture exists always, not just during a certain holiday or season. People in the Chinese community don't just buy things during Lunar New Year! Seasonal holidays and celebrations are great opportunities to connect culturally, but they shouldn't be a replacement for connecting culturally every single day.

V is for Validate. Ask "Why?" five times. Are you sure this is conveying exactly what you want to convey? Are you sure it's the right image, the right phrase, the right product? Are you sure you have the right customer experience? Are you sure you've trained your frontline staff in how to respectfully and effectively communicate with different cultures? Are you sure? Are you sure?

C is for Connect Through Culture (Not Just Ethnicity). You can connect through any and all of the facets of the culture wheel; don't get stuck on skin colour!

Living with families to see how they use products, attending cultural events, seeking out a guide to help you achieve greater immersion and understanding—all of this is anthropology. Of course, all of these involve way more time and effort. Going to a festival takes more time and personal commitment than simply checking a box or typing a question into ChatGPT. As we've discussed, culture moves very quickly today; going deeper is about slowing down and taking the time to immerse, understand, and connect. You can't rush it. You have to be patient.

Going deeper is about discovering your own humanity and the humanity of others. It's easy to look at someone and say, "You fit into this box." The Multicultural Mindset requires a deeper understanding, which takes more time, discussion, and debate. You need to invest the time to understand, to put yourself in the shoes of other people with the goal of understanding cultures and communities outside of your own sphere. It takes longer—but in the end, you will always have better results and a deeper, more genuine connection with humanity.

KEY TAKEAWAYS

→ Asking "Why?" five times will lead to deeper, more authentic understanding.

→ Multiculturalism is more than skin colour and language.

→ If you want to truly understand and experience another culture–and if you want to increase your MQ–you need to get offline and immerse IRL.

→ Your exposure needs to be more than cursory; no single voice or experience of a culture can adequately represent the perspective of millions. Real cultural understanding requires investment and remembering the AVCs: Always On, Validate, and Connect Through Culture (Not Just Ethnicity).

CHAPTER 6

THE FEAR FACTOR

"When working across cultures, we must be aware of our own cultural biases and be willing to challenge and adapt them."

–Erin Meyer

Fear acts as an inhibitor to building a Multicultural Mindset and affects us as individuals, teams, and organizations. I want to acknowledge an important truth: Going deeper into cultural understanding can be frightening, and what we're experiencing in these moments of hesitation isn't just personal fear—it's what researchers call "cultural inertia," a natural resistance to cultural change that affects us all, even when that change might benefit us.[69]

---

69 Michael A. Zárate and Moira P. Shaw, "The Role of Cultural Inertia in Reactions to Immigration on the US/Mexico Border," *Journal of Social Issues* 66, no. 1 (March 2010): 45–57, https://www.researchgate.net/publication/229466986_The_Role_of_Cultural_Inertia_in_Reactions_to_Immigration_on_the_USMexico_Border.

UNDERSTANDING OUR RESISTANCE TO FEAR

Humans naturally resist cultural change, even when we consciously know it could be beneficial. It's not just you—it's a fundamental human characteristic, rooted in our evolutionary tribal survival instinct that Michael Morris talks about in *Tribal*.[70] Think of cultural inertia as a powerful magnet, constantly pulling us back toward our familiar cultural patterns and practices. This explains why humans naturally like to stick with what is familiar and comfortable—and why change feels so uncomfortable.

However, in my experience, growth in a borderless world can only happen when you push against this natural resistance. This resistance operates on both individual and institutional levels, creating what researchers call a "cultural comfort zone"—a space where we feel secure but which can limit our growth and understanding.[71]

Let me share a story that illustrates this concept.

On a Filipino news program during a recent election period, I heard an elderly Filipina woman who had immigrated to the US talking about supporting policies and a candidate that were against immigration itself.

Her rationale?

She had fought hard to get where she was, and she didn't want others—namely other immigrants—to take from her what she had worked so hard to accomplish.

This attitude is driven by cultural inertia, and that resistance is exactly what political movements and leaders often tap into during times of growth and change.

---

70   Morris, *Tribal*.

71   M. J. Bennett, "Becoming Interculturally Competent," in *Toward Multiculturalism: A Reader in Multicultural Education* (Intercultural Resource Corporation, 2004), https://www.idrinstitute.org/wp-content/uploads/2018/02/becoming_ic_competent.pdf.

What's interesting to me, and perhaps to many others, is that this phenomenon still occurs where people who have achieved success within a system become resistant to changes in that system, even when those changes mirror their own path.[72]

And it hits close to home. The Filipina woman's words also mirrored a similar conversation I had with my own family members who had immigrated to Canada. Recent changes in political leadership in Canada and massive changes in immigration policy have certainly been making my own family dinners and conversations uncomfortable.

GET COMFORTABLE BEING UNCOMFORTABLE

Part of building a Multicultural Mindset is becoming comfortable with being uncomfortable. It will never be a set-and-forget situation. You constantly need to be curious and learning and open to challenging your comfort zone.

A mentor and former boss of mine, Juan Carlos Blanco—or JC for short—taught me this lesson in a way I will always remember!

One sunny day, at a leadership retreat in King City, Canada, I was confronted with literally my worst fear: heights. Factor in gravity and my sizable body weight ... I simply stayed away from anything involving dangling or plummeting to the ground. Ski lifts, Ferris wheels, and suspension bridges all made me super uncomfortable.

The challenge? To scale a thirty-foot pole and jump off the top while touching a ball suspended in the air. Granted, there were safety provisions: a harness, a helmet, and a spotting team of two or more

---

72   Julia Bourke, "The Diversity and Inclusion Revolution: Eight Powerful Truths," Deloitte Insights, January 22, 2018, https://www2.deloitte.com/us/en/insights/deloitte-review/issue-22/diversity-and-inclusion-at-work-eight-powerful-truths.html.

teammates. I watched as teammates scaled the pole like Spider-Man. I also watched a few team members tap out completely and spot only. It took me a good two hours into the activity to build up the courage to strap on the harness.

"What the fuck am I doing?" I muttered to myself as I scaled the full-size ladder and then made my way to the pole. Somewhere around the top, and several expletives later, I hovered like the cherry on top of an ice cream cone, shouting, "I can't do this!"

But JC yelled at me, "Just go for it, JD! We got you."

So I did. I reached for the ball and tried to hoist myself up … and missed my mark. I felt myself falling through the air, and my teammates, four of them at this point—strong, burly men—had my safety rope in hand.

I had never faced my fear of heights until that day. And it took a leader plus a team to help me through it. Thanks, JC!

FEAR IS NORMAL

The physical manifestation of fear is something I felt that day, and as I learned, it is completely normal. We can all take consolation in the fact that we are not alone in feeling it. Naturally, when humans are confronted with something that scares them, they go into fight-or-flight mode. And this can often be the case in addressing one's own Multicultural Mindset.

Even if you have already started to build your Multicultural Mindset—even if you are MQ Blue—you will still likely encounter fear and discomfort. Even if you absolutely love to travel and experience new cultures, perhaps you still feel a little nervous navigating countries where you don't speak the language. That's completely normal! Even the most open, multicultural-minded person is bound to feel some discomfort or nervousness—or even fear—confronting the unknown. That is simply part of being human.

Fear of the unknown or going out of your personal comfort zone leads to inaction and apathy—not increasing your knowledge, not seeking new experiences outside your own sphere, not taking action. If you give in to your fear of the unknown, you'll end up only focusing on things that are in your circle, which reinforces tunnel vision and the negative effects of tribalism we discussed in chapter 1. After all, if everyone in your sphere is behaving that way, then you come to think of it as normal.

A DIGITAL PARADOX TO CONFRONTING FEAR

Many people may not even realize that fear can be the catalyst or detractor in building their MQ both personally and professionally. Today, as a society, we are so conditioned to be comfortable—just as I had always avoided my fear of heights. The instinct to fight doesn't come naturally anymore.

Before the internet age, when we wanted to learn about something, we needed to go to a library, find a book, take down notes, and process the information. These steps were time-consuming, yes—but they also built up resiliency and MQ. In fact, studies have shown that effortful learning increases retention.[73] The very friction in the process builds cognitive resilience.

Today's instant access to information has fundamentally changed how we process new ideas and perspectives. Microsoft's attention research reveals a startling trend: Our average attention span dropped from twelve seconds in 2000 to eight seconds in 2015.[74] This shortened attention span particularly affects our ability to engage with complex cultural concepts that require sustained focus and reflection.

Even more concerning, researchers have found that easy access to information online creates an "illusion of understanding"—people

---

73   Art Kohn, "Brain Science: Should Learning Be Easy? How Effortful Processing Improves Retention," Learning Guild, September 17, 2014, https://www.Learning-Guild.com/articles/1502/brain-science-should-learning-be-easy-how-effortful-processing-improves-retention/.

74   "Attention Spans," Consumer Insights, Microsoft Canada, Spring 2015, https://dl.motamem.org/microsoft-attention-spans-research-report.pdf.

overestimating their knowledge or understanding.[75] This false confidence can be particularly problematic when dealing with cultural differences, where surface-level understanding often masquerades as true comprehension.

This is the paradox of our digital age: While information about different cultures is more accessible than ever, our psychological resistance to cultural engagement has become more subtle and entrenched, resulting in digital cultural isolation.

OVERCOMING THAT FEAR OF F***ING UP

Let's face it. We all fear making a mistake. But what happens when that mistake gets you cancelled? Or fired?

This fear isn't just personal—it's deeply rooted in what Michael Morris identifies as our tribal survival instinct, a psychological mechanism that evolved to protect us from social exclusion and group rejection. When we venture into unfamiliar cultural territory, our tribal mind activates what neuroscientists call the "behavioural inhibition system"—our internal alarm that makes us hesitate, withdraw, or disengage.[76] This explains why even well-intentioned efforts to engage with different cultures can feel physically uncomfortable.

When confronting biases—whether our own or others'—our tribal mind pushes us to avoid conflict, basically for fear of f***ing up.

It's hard to lean in to things we don't understand—and be brave enough to ask questions about what we don't know without fear of looking stupid or ignorant. It takes great humility to say "I don't

---

75   Jeroen de Ridder, "Online Illusions of Understanding," *Social Epistemology* 38, no. 6 (December 28, 2022): 727–42, https://doi.org/10.1080/02691728.2022.2151331.

76   Shelly L. Gable, Harry T. Reis, and Andrew J. Elliot, "Behavioral Activation and Inhibition in Everyday Life," *Journal of Personality and Social Psychology* 78, no. 6 (2000): 1135–49, https://doi.org/10.1037/0022-3514.78.6.1135.

know" or "I don't understand." It also takes great humility to face the internal biases we may not be aware of, which may come to light when we step out of our comfort zone and into a cultural sphere with which we are unfamiliar. When someone calls us out on our behaviour or unconscious bias, it can be incredibly painful. It is very tempting to resist, to put walls up, to become even more rigidly stuck in our ways. Instead, I invite us to consider these moments as opportunities to open ourselves, to pivot, and to see new things about ourselves, the people around us, and the world.

MY FIGHT-THE-FEAR CHEERLEADER

During times of fear, you need a cheerleader or a coach in the workplace. And for me, that person was Chito Gonzalez.

A respected sales and business development officer at Western Union, Chito was thirty years my senior and a fellow Filipino colleague. His ability to build relationships with key government agents and community leaders made him a vital part of our team. He taught me the importance of pushing past our tribal mind, and he did it with MQ Blue-level mastery.

In 2008, I had just delivered my son. After a painful miscarriage and loss two years prior, my body and my professional mindset were running on fumes. Having worked in corporate marketing, I was always a strong individual contributor and a very reluctant leader, especially now that I was a new mom.

I was, simply put, very content to play it safe in roles that were in my comfort zone. Then, while I was still on maternity leave, a leadership opportunity was presented to me: to lead the whole Canadian team. Chito flew from Toronto to chilly and snowy Edmonton to visit me.

"You need to lead the team, Joycelyn," he said after we had enjoyed a home-cooked meal of our Filipino sinigang (tamarind-based Filipino stew).

"But I *just* had a baby! And we don't want to move to Toronto," I retorted. "Plus, the team is too different from me, and I really don't think I can make the changes needed." Clearly, at this point, I was still MQ Yellow—maybe MQ Red!

Chito sat there on my sofa thinking, looking at my son Lorenzo wrapped up like a lumpia in my arms.

"I say this with all the love, like you are my daughter," he said. "Stop being so Filipino! You are more than a hard worker. You're already doing the job of the leader, Joycelyn. Why not get the pay and recognition for it—for you and your son?"

I was stunned. *What do you mean stop being so Filipino?* I thought to myself. I later understood his meaning to be more about keeping my head down, demure and collectivist. He wanted me to fight my fear and embrace the change.

But in that moment, he simply uttered, "Kaya mo to"—Tagalog for: You got this.

And that was all I needed to hear, in Tagalog, to muster myself to fight the fear of the unknown city, unknown job, and unknown adventure ahead.

So yes, after three months on a very short maternity leave, I became the leader of the product and marketing team for Canada. And it was thanks to Chito's MQ Blue mastery, his understanding of the cultural cues of my background and professional experience, plus the time he took to personally and in real life appeal across the aisle to help me out of my comfort zone and fear of leadership.

I'm eternally grateful to Chito for sharing that bowl of sinigang with me and my son. It was the catalyst to grow my own MQ and multicultural leadership.

As a new leader in a national role, I now had a lot more to fear. I needed to use my voice and conquer my fear of speaking up.

FACING THE FEAR OF SPEAKING UP

Let's talk about something that hits close to home for many of us.

You know that gut-wrenching feeling when you're suddenly the only one in the room who looks like you? For folks used to being in the majority, this can feel like being thrown in at the deep end. But here's the thing—that uncomfortable feeling? It's actually a gift in disguise. It's giving you a tiny glimpse into what many people experience every single day of their lives. The experience of being a minority in any space creates a unique form of psychological tension and fear of speaking up.

Now, let's talk about the elephant in the room—speaking up when we witness bias. Whether it's a "harmless" joke, a subtle dig, or outright discrimination, we've all been in situations where we knew something wasn't right. The questions start racing through our minds: Should I say something? What if I make it worse? What if I lose my job? What if I'm misreading the situation?

The same can be true of the other side of this interaction—calling someone out on their biases. If you witness racism, bigotry, or sexism—do you call it out? Do you speak up for the person who is being discriminated against? Do you try to educate the person who acted in this way, to help them expand their mindset? Do you try to close the gap between the differing perspectives? If your answer is no, that's OK—it is not an easy thing to do. In fact, it can be quite scary!

I get it. I really do. It's like standing at the edge of a diving board—the longer you stand there, the scarier it gets. (Remember—I am afraid of heights!)

But here's what I've learned through my work with People of Colour in Advertising and Marketing (POCAM): Silence has its own cost. When we recently surveyed people of colour in the advertising industry, a staggering 77 percent reported experiencing microaggressions in their organizations. Behind that number are real people, real careers, real lives being affected every single day.[77]

But—and this is important—this isn't about shame or guilt. It's about growth. Every time I've pushed past that fear to speak up, even when my voice was shaking, I learned something valuable. Sometimes I stumbled, sometimes I didn't get it quite right, but each time it got a little easier.

Research actually backs this up—it turns out our brains are pretty amazing at adapting when we push through discomfort.[78] It's like building a muscle. The first workout is tough, but stick with it, and suddenly you're lifting weights you never thought possible.

Here's what I want you to remember: You don't have to be perfect at this. You just have to be willing to try. Whether you're experiencing being in the minority for the first time or gathering the courage to speak up against bias, every step forward counts. Even small actions create ripples—when one person speaks up, it often gives others the courage to do the same.[79]

---

77   "State of Diversity in Canadian Advertising and Marketing: Annual Report," POCAM, 2023.

78   Nicole Spector, "How to Train Your Brain to Accept Change, According to Neuroscience," NBC News, November 12, 2018, https://www.nbcnews.com/better/health/how-train-your-brain-accept-change-according-neuroscience-ncna934011.

79   Derald Wing Sue, "Race Talk: The Psychology of Racial Dialogues," *The American Psychologist* 68, no. 8 (November 2013): 663–72, https://doi.org/10.1037/a0033681.

Research shows that organizations where people consistently speak up against bias show measurably better outcomes:

- Higher employee retention rates

- Increased innovation and creativity

- Stronger financial performance

- More effective problem-solving capabilities[80]

The key lies in recognizing that discomfort with speaking up is natural but not insurmountable. Each time we choose to push through this discomfort, we're not just addressing individual instances of bias—we're helping to reshape organizational culture.

FROM INDIVIDUAL CHANGE TO ORGANIZATIONAL TRANSFORMATION

How can groups of humans, in companies or communities, address their fear factor together at scale? Fear operates on both individual and institutional levels, creating what researchers call a "cultural comfort zone"—a space where we feel secure but which can limit our growth and understanding.[81]

The whole marketing industry has been predicated on driving culture forward and being innovative. But what does that mean in today's multicultural, global, borderless world? It means you have to be relevant—and leaders have to face fears organizationally and be brave. Is it brave to do a TikTok dance that everyone is doing? Probably not. But if you reframe it—if you put, say, an Inuit woman

---

80   "Why Diversity Matters Even More," McKinsey & Company.

81   Michelle Ami Reyes, "The Problem of Cultural Comfort Zones," *Medium* (blog), May 6, 2021, https://medium.com/ar-che-type/the-problem-of-cultural-comfort-zones-cd54dc077738.

doing that TikTok dance from the beauty of her homeland, that just might be brave.

It takes bravery to dig deeper. It takes getting a little uncomfortable. It may even take some painful moments of encountering your own internal biases.

But bravery at an organizational level is a bit more nuanced.

The fear of making a mistake or being misinterpreted or accidentally offending someone, or a consumer group, when you do step out of your comfort zone halts a lot of people in their tracks. When we make mistakes, it can be easy to say, "Well, we tried and we messed it up, so we're not going to try again." Again, this comes from a place of fear—but the truth is, you have already overcome fear once by taking action and trying it in the first place. In fact, if you mess up, the worst thing you can do is say, "Let's not ever do that again."

One of the best things you can do to overcome this fear is to have an advisor or ally at your side, whether that's someone from that culture who brings you in and shows you around, like my friend Ranbir, or an expert consultant or advisor who specializes in multicultural markets and can coach you. This is often what AVC does—we are brought on when there has been a mistake, and we create a risk management plan to avoid mistakes in the future.

The AVC Model from chapter 5, like the Multicultural Mindset overall, is only effective in an organization if the *whole* organization is behind it.

Sometimes, there are people within organizations who want to be agents of change but are afraid to stand up or speak out because the organization feels unwelcoming to those perspectives. I've seen the passion for change die out in an organization, purely through osmosis—the attitude of the organization as a whole imbuing the individual.

Apathy at an institutional level can easily drown out individual passion. I've seen it happen over and over. I worked with a brand for which my point person was someone who had transferred from an organization's office in Nigeria to the office in Canada. When they arrived at the Canadian office, they were full of passion, of fire, of plans. Within a year, through osmosis, that passion and fire died, because everyone around them was saying, "That's just not how we do things here."

It proved to me that you can't just hire people with Multicultural Mindsets; your whole organization has to have a Multicultural Mindset, from the top executive levels to the managers and supervisors all the way to the frontline employees. There has to be an organizational environment that embraces diverse perspectives and doesn't quash employees' passions. The organization as a whole has to have a Multicultural Mindset.

Why doesn't this happen? Because change at an institutional level requires bold leadership steeped in MQ. It's much less scary to just tread water and uphold the status quo. But from a business perspective, it's a failure to act on a market opportunity. I see it all the time—brands fail to lean into opportunities that are right in front of their faces.

But not all organizations fall prey to the fear. Some are overcoming it with a focus on building MQ at every level.

BREAKING THROUGH: WHEN ORGANIZATIONS FACE THEIR FEARS

I worked with a brand that confessed that it didn't have the resources to invest in creating a Chinese language landing page to receive its customers—but it wanted to reach the Chinese community. "We only have English and French landing pages available," the client told me. "Is that going to offend the Chinese community?" The brand was truly afraid of reaching out to the Chinese community because it did not have a Chinese language landing page.

"It won't offend that community," I reassured the client. "It is not offensive to expect people who immigrate to this country to be familiar with English or French. However, if you market to them, take the time to at least be able to say 'hello' to them in their language of comfort. Bring them in the door with that gesture of understanding and connection. Then, feel free to service them in English or French. You won't offend them. But if you can reach them in their language of comfort, you are going to stand out in the crowd."

I have had so many conversations with clients who were afraid to even start a multicultural initiative because they were worried they wouldn't be able to do enough. But you have to take that first step— and I'm here to tell you that however far the first step takes you is OK. What's important is taking the leap.

Again, this is where a guide can be invaluable. An experienced guide can say, "This is where you should start." Bringing in a multicultural expert is no different from bringing in an expert to consult on any other market segment—something companies do all the time. Most companies will invest in market research, but many will overlook researching new and emerging audiences, which are often multicultural.

Understanding cultural inertia is one thing; actively working to overcome it is another challenge entirely. While many organizations acknowledge the importance of cultural adaptation, the gap between recognition and action often remains wide. Yet some organizations have found the courage to push through this resistance, transforming their fear of cultural missteps into catalysts for innovation. Their stories offer valuable lessons about what happens when institutions decide to face their fears head-on.

The Beauty Brand Revolution

A global beauty brand took an even bolder step. Facing declining market share despite increasing diversity in its target markets, its transformation went beyond surface-level changes. It established dedicated R&D teams focusing on multicultural beauty needs, completely rebuilt its marketing teams to reflect target demographics, and engaged cultural influencers not just as ambassadors but as partners in product development. This comprehensive approach addressed what organizational psychologists call "structural inertia"—the tendency of established processes to resist fundamental change.[82]

Beyond Marketing—Growth Through Market Transformation

Loblaw Companies Ltd.'s journey with T&T Supermarket demonstrates the long-term commitment required for true cultural transformation. What began as an acquisition in 2009 evolved into a comprehensive lesson in cultural adaptation. Growing from seventeen to thirty-three stores across Canada, the company didn't just expand—it fundamentally changed how mainstream Canadian retail approaches cultural diversity.[83]

---

82   Michael T. Hannan and John Freeman, "Structural Inertia and Organizational Change," *American Sociological Review* 49, no. 2 (April 1984): 149–64, https://doi.org/10.2307/2095567.

83   "Annual Information Form," Loblaw Companies Limited, February 22, 2024, https://dis-prod.assetful.loblaw.ca/content/dam/loblaw-companies-limited/creative-assets/loblaw-ca/investor-relations-reports/annual/2023/Loblaw%20Annual%20Information%20form%202023_EN.pdf.

Fantuan's Disruptive Innovation

Perhaps the most compelling recent example comes from Fantuan, the Vancouver-based food delivery platform. Unlike traditional companies adapting to cultural diversity, Fantuan built its entire business model around cultural understanding. Its success—expanding to more than fifty cities and recently closing a $40 million Series C funding round—challenges traditional assumptions about "niche" markets.[84]

There are countless examples and case studies that give me hope, but it still feels as though more needs to be done. I once had a brand tell me its reason for ignoring multicultural consumers was "because everyone is our audience. We don't need to do multicultural targeting. We can just reach everybody." But when you try to reach everybody at the same time, you end up with an incredibly generic, vanilla, uninteresting ad. When you try to reach everybody, you reach nobody. There's no stickiness. There's no moment of, "You see me."

FROM FEAR TO MQ IN YOUR ORGANIZATION

It's also important to remember that not all multicultural agencies or consultants are equal. Many bring their own bias into their work and don't necessarily have the frameworks or processes to execute nuanced multicultural initiatives, instead operating on a surface level. This is also dangerous, because it makes it easy to think, "Well, the guide will take care of it. I don't have to pay attention." This is why the Multicultural Mindset needs to exist within the organization as well, at every level.

---

84   "Fantuan Raises $40 Million Series C Round, Led by E-Commerce Platform Grub-Market," Canada Newswire, December 5, 2023, https://www.newswire.ca/news-releases/fantuan-raises-40-million-series-c-round-led-by-e-commerce-platform-grubmarket-807553120.html.

The Multicultural Mindset says: See the fear, acknowledge it, and do it anyway. It's about being open to engaging and learning with the intent of understanding.

Remember that MQ exists already in your organization and is evolving every day, not just during specific holidays or cultural events. Your Multicultural Mindset needs to be always on, which means investing in building your MQ every day.

As we've discussed in previous chapters, you can't base any business, product, or marketing strategy in one aspect of the culture wheel, be it language or otherwise, and expect it to represent the entirety of a culture. This is where mistakes often happen. Put in due diligence and do the research. The more points of interaction you have, the more opportunity you have to test and learn and build up your knowledge through experience.

Another tool to validate nuanced multicultural work is marketing audits. A CPG brand we audited had been working with a mainstream media agency to target Southeast Asian people in Canada. But the ad campaign it created leaned into Indian culture and language—and India is not part of Southeast Asia! The whole campaign the media agency created was targeting the wrong audience. It wasn't until AVC did a marketing audit that the error was caught—and, of course, fixed.

Lastly, and something we will explore in chapter 8, you cannot just validate by asking Google or ChatGPT. Google or ChatGPT would not have caught the issues in all those advertising mistakes we discussed in chapter 4. But if Heinz or Tesco had taken the time to validate, to test those advertisements or products with a focus group in the community, they likely would have gotten feedback and been able to adjust their campaigns—and would have avoided the public backlash and humiliation they faced.

KEY TAKEAWAYS

→ Fear is normal. A Multicultural Mindset isn't about not being afraid; it's about seeing that fear, acknowledging it, and then doing it anyway!

→ One of the best ways to overcome fear is to have an advisor or ally at your side.

→ Facing our fears is something we can do on an individual level—and an institutional level.

CHAPTER 7

FOSTERING MULTICULTURAL COMMUNICATION AND CONNECTION

"Cultural intelligence is the new EQ. Understanding and navigating different tribal cultures–whether in global business or diverse teams–is becoming a crucial leadership skill."

–Michael Morris

uilding genuine connections across cultures often seems deceptively simple yet proves surprisingly complex in practice. The challenge lies not only in bridging obvious differences but also in navigating the subtle nuances of cultural communication.

In my experience, connection often comes when you least expect it. As a member of various leadership teams over the years, I've sat in a lot of management meetings. Often, I am the only woman in the room—so I sometimes struggle to find points of connection with peers or clients. Should I talk about hockey? Maybe soccer? The weather—that's always safe, right?

At one such meeting where all the business heads of the major divisions came together to share business highlights, I was in attendance because my boss was running late after another meeting. During the pre-meeting banter, the division heads would typically chat about sports and the usual, "How's your wife? How're your kids?" etc.

The president was surprised to see me. "Oh, Joycelyn, you're here?" he said.

"Yeah," I said. "Great to see you!"

"How are you today?" he asked.

"Wonderful, thank you!"

And then, after a brief pause, he said, "I haven't seen you in a while. Your hair looks different from the last time I saw you."

I was slightly taken aback; it seemed odd that he would ask about my hair. "Well, yeah," I said, "I got a haircut."

"Oh, cool," he said. I thought that was it, but then he continued. "It looks very different. Have you been doing something different with it?"

Why the heck is he asking me all these questions about my hair in front of twenty division heads? I thought. Out loud, I said, "Oh, well, as I'm getting older, I need to make it easier to style, you know."

Once again, I thought that was the end—but once again, he wouldn't let it go. For a full two minutes, he asked me about my hair care regimen, how I style it, how long it takes. Meanwhile, the men in the room were just sitting there watching this exchange. I was mortified—though I didn't show it.

Finally, my boss, walked in. "You know who has a new haircut?" I said. "Check him out!"

The room erupted into laughter—because my boss did, in fact, have a shiny new haircut. That diffused the situation, and we proceeded to move on to the business of the meeting. But the entire meeting, I sat there processing, wondering why the president had spent *so long* talking about my hair.

Finally, I realized: He was trying to make a connection. He was from a South American culture, where the norm is to find a point of connection through personal details. While North American culture might favour small talk about the weather before moving on to business, in the president's culture, you show respect and politeness by connecting on a personal level. He was trying to connect with me as a woman and thought talking about my hair would be a good way to do that.

While I was somewhat offended and mortified in the moment, upon reflection, I understood that it was simply a different style of communication, a different way of trying to establish a rapport. My approach, my style, was to diffuse the situation with humour. I then tried to imagine what I would do if the script were flipped.

What if I was talking to the only man in a room full of women? Or what if it was a different scenario—what if someone was the only Asian person in a room full of English and French speakers, and they didn't know the language? In all of these situations, you would want to find a point of connection—whether that's talking about sports or the weather or, yes, even a haircut.

Whenever I tell this story to women, they always agree that they would have found it mortifying as well. But when I share it with men—especially men from certain cultures in Latin America— they say, "Yes, that makes sense—we like to celebrate our women!" It all comes down to understanding the differences in how cultures communicate.

UNDERSTANDING CROSS-CULTURAL COMMUNICATION

How do you prepare for the different cultural communication styles you might encounter?

Both Hofstede and Meyer provide frameworks for understanding how communication styles differ in different countries. Hofstede found that in China, people tend to be more literal and authoritative, while in Latin America, people tend to be more expressive. These frameworks offer valuable starting points, but today's reality is more complex. In our Multicultural Era, we're dealing with fluid, overlapping cultural identities rather than rigid categories. Understanding this complexity is crucial for effective communication.

These frameworks individually are a great starting point from which to begin practising cross-cultural communication. However, it's important to remember that while Hofstede positioned cultural dimensions as separate spheres—this country and culture over here, that country and culture over there—today, in our multicultural and globally connected multiverse, we are living in a Multicultural Era where everything is in motion. Meyer studied what happens when these cultures interact in a business environment—and what happens when they clash with each other.

When I find out someone's background, I have in my head what Hofstede and Meyer say about that culture's communication style. Of course, not everyone directly aligns with their cultural background, and as we have discussed, most people exist in multiple cultural spheres. But this knowledge gives me a place to start, to say, "OK, they're more likely to communicate in this style." Or, if I know a person was born into one culture but raised in another, I can think about how those two cultural communication styles might blend.

And, just as importantly, I can think about my own communication style and how it might interact with that person's communication style. You have to be aware of yourself and educate yourself about the other person and/or the environment you are in. In the story I shared above, I was working with predominantly Latino colleagues. When I started, I had no point of connection to or deeper awareness of that culture. Being in a global company really put the theories of Hofstede and Meyer into practice!

Early in my career, I attended a training session where the trainer talked about the different communication styles of introverts and extroverts. He explained the difference between introverts and extroverts—which, contrary to what you might think, has nothing to do with being shy or being outgoing. An extrovert goes to a party or to a bar, socializes, and gets totally energized by this, ready to go to the after-party. An introvert does the same—with the same level of social skill—and then needs to go home and be by themselves to recharge. Extroverts draw energy from others; introverts draw energy from within. This was the moment when I realized I was naturally an introvert (though I have learned to navigate toward ambivert!).

Understand Yourself to Understand Others

Developing my own Multicultural Mindset and MQ began with first understanding myself and then taking the time and intention to really know what the baseline is for different colleagues or people I interact with. I've learned to avoid cultural communication blind spots—even though they are not always easy to see!

My first blind spot was learning from my own cultural bias. When the acquisition opportunity for AVC presented itself, I learned firsthand about the danger of one's own bias and cultural assumptions. In 2018, I quit my job, got a tattoo, moved my family across the country—and bought the business that would become AVC, a leading multicultural marketing agency.

But I let my bias and implicit trust in the cultural norms of Filipino culture get the better of me. Working in an all-Filipino business environment actually resulted in my latent and lax approach to doing due diligence, which caused me to miss important elements and nuances of the transaction.

With hindsight, I set out to put my Multicultural Mindset to work!

I knew I needed to make the best of the situation and start working to turn the company into what I believed it could be. First, I listened to and learned the communication and work styles of every member of my team. We were a small team back then, only eight people, so this was totally feasible—and also revealing.

I had two people on my team, a media planner and an account manager, who just could not work together. Unfortunately, their jobs required them to—but they could not seem to figure out how to communicate with each other in any format. One would write long emails that the other would not read; one would call the other, and the other would respond by booking a meeting. The form of communication—email, text, chat, in person—didn't matter. They just could not communicate.

Over time, this problem started to escalate. They were working together on an account, so of course they needed to be able to communicate—but it just wasn't happening. Fingers started to be pointed: "They're not listening to me," "They're not understanding what I'm saying." I heard endless complaints from both sides—and endless complaints from their managers. I knew I had to see if I could understand what was happening. Was it miscommunication? Was it a fundamental misalignment on understanding what needed to happen to get the job done?

I looked closely at the situation and quickly realized: It all boiled down to a lack of understanding of how to effectively communicate across cultures. The media planner was originally from Hong Kong and had only recently started working in Canada. As petite as a ballerina, she spoke Chinese, with English as her second language, and was extremely conscientious and responsible as a media planner. The account manager was a Latino man who was full of vivacious energy and wit as sharp as a razor. This was what made him an excellent client services professional, and I valued his experience with clients (something I did not have as a new agency owner).

If you look at the communication styles of these cultures on a map of the world, they couldn't be more opposite. One is more expressive; one is more formal. One is more "Let's just understand the data and make a decision with as little discussion as possible"; one is more, "Let's talk about this and debate it for five hours." Once I realized this, I sat down with each of them individually and walked through their communication style, using the Hofstede framework and asking, "Does this sound like you and the way you prefer to communicate?"

"Actually, it does," they said. "This and this, maybe not so much this, but that and that—overall, it tracks."

Then, I took the style information from each of them and swapped it—giving the opposite person's profile to each. "Take a look at this," I said to them. "This is how the other person likes to communicate."

It was like a light bulb went off. "Oh, that's so different from me!" they each said. "I didn't think about that!"

By first asking them to understand and acknowledge their own communication styles and then asking them to understand the other person's—both of which were culturally driven by their unique individual backgrounds—they were able to see that there was actually no personal animosity between them. It was simply a matter of different communication styles!

Chinese and Latino communication styles are about as opposite as you can get. But in order to work together, neither person had to change their communication style. They simply had to be aware of each other's style and understand where the other person was coming from, have a mutual understanding of what the other preferred and make some accommodations to come a little closer together.

I gave each of these team members a few things to do differently—and their communication difficulties cleared up. It didn't happen overnight; this whole process took about three months. But by the end of it, not only were they able to work effectively together— they were workplace besties!

Until I sat them down, asked them to understand and acknowledge themselves then asked them to understand and acknowledge each other, they had never thought to examine their cultural communication styles. Often, when you have people who don't like to work with each other, who don't get along, it stems from some kind of failure to communicate. This happens all the time in corporations. And often, that miscommunication is a result of—or exacerbated by—a lack of cultural context and understanding. A little bit of understanding of where you are and where the other person is can help build effective communication. And, in fact, it was this exercise I did with these two people that formed the basis of what would become the MQ assessment you took at the start of this book!

As an entrepreneur navigating real business challenges, it's easy to get tunnel vision. "I need to make a plan," "I need to close that account," or "I need to keep staff on during the pandemic." Part of developing my Multicultural Mindset was rooted in being willing to cross that line, to get out of my own bubble and better understand the suppliers, employees, and communities that are unlike my own style.

When unaddressed, communication problems can lead to far bigger problems. Often, especially in global and/or diverse companies, these communication problems can be sorted simply by understanding differences in communication styles on an individual level.

Fortunately for me, adopting the Multicultural Mindset led to success. In five years, we expanded our business fivefold, and employee retention skyrocketed to over 90 percent!

The Multicultural Mindset is about embracing our own autonomy and our own agency. What can we do at an individual level? To begin with, we can understand ourselves. Then, we can cross that barrier and understand others.

Diversity Is Good for Business (Now Repeat That Again)

"Diversity is good for business" has become a common refrain—and it is not without its detractors. While I personally have witnessed throughout my career the positive business impact a diverse team and mindset can bring, I acknowledge that the challenges extend far beyond simple demographics or training programs. Unconscious bias workshops and cultural sensitivity training may provide important foundations, but research consistently shows these initiatives alone often yield diminishing returns over time.[85]

The path to lasting change requires something deeper: a mindset shift—and constant repetition!

"Diversity is good for business." I find myself repeating this during meetings, conferences, and podcasts as a reminder to audiences. I also usually add, "And let's be clear, diversity goes beyond the colour of

---

85   Frank Dobbin and Alexandra Kalev, "Why Diversity Programs Fail," *Harvard Business Review*, July 1, 2016, https://hbr.org/2016/07/why-diversity-programs-fail.

your skin or the language you speak. Diversity is a multiverse. And whether you like it or not, we are in it."

Tough Truths

I discovered some hard truths during the pandemic while hosting virtual sessions with Nick Noorani on the short-lived platform Clubhouse. Connecting with newcomers to Canada every week, we heard story after story of the real cost of cultural blindness in our organizations. An accomplished software engineer from Shanghai confided she was considering adopting an English name just to secure interviews. A senior project manager from Ireland, with fifteen years of experience, kept hearing the same refrain: "Sorry, you lack Canadian experience." These weren't isolated incidents—they represented a systemic failure to recognize and value diverse perspectives.

Recent data from the Institute for Canadian Citizenship (ICC) confirms what we were hearing anecdotally. Their comprehensive study, conducted with the Conference Board of Canada, revealed an alarming trend: Highly skilled immigrants are leaving Canada at unprecedented rates.[86]

"These are tradespeople who build our homes, nurses who care for our loved ones, truckers who facilitate commerce, and entrepreneurs who spur innovation," said ICC CEO Daniel Bernhard. "And they are increasingly headed out the door. Canadians are bombarded with commentary telling them that high immigration levels are to blame for homegrown challenges including housing supply, inaccessible healthcare, crime, and even traffic."

---

86   Stein Monteiro, Federica Guccini, and Lauren Hamman, "The Leaky Bucket 2024: A Closer Look at Immigrant Onward Migration in Canada," The Conference Board of Canada, November 19, 2024, https://inclusion.ca/wp-content/uploads/2024/11/the-leaky-bucket_2024.pdf.

"Be careful what you wish for," Bernhard cautioned. "This is globally coveted talent with global options. We need programs that entice them to stay, become active citizens, and help fuel our economy."[87]

This exodus carries profound implications. BCG's research demonstrates that companies with diverse leadership teams generate 19 percent higher innovation revenue than their more homogeneous counterparts.[88] Similarly, diverse organizations earn two and a half times higher cash flow per employee.[89]

Yet, despite these compelling numbers, many organizations struggle to move beyond surface-level diversity initiatives. Why? Because they lack a leader with MQ to champion it!

When you have a leader with high MQ as a business champion, they are also able to see things others might not. Remember the H&M case study from chapter 3? That campaign never would have come into being if the general manager had not had experience working in China. His knowledge, his experience, his MQ, allowed him to see an opportunity that otherwise would have been missed. The Multicultural Mindset allows you to see opportunities others can't see and to see and address people issues or product issues you might not be able to see without that expanded worldview.

A Multicultural Mindset means having a fundamental understanding that your place in the world is just one of many places in the

87   "Economic Immigrants Hand-Picked by the Federal Government Are Leading a Growing Exodus of Newcomers from Canada," Institute for Canadian Citizenship, November 19, 2024, https://inclusion.ca/article/economic-immigrants-hand-picked-by-the-federal-government-are-leading-a-growing-exodus-of-newcomers-from-canada/.

88   Lorenzo et al., "Diverse Leadership."

89   Darpan Munjal, "The Unexpected Power of Outsiders in Building Innovative Teams," *Forbes*, January 21, 2025, https://www.forbes.com/sites/darpanmunjal/2025/01/21/the-unexpected-power-of-outsiders-in-building-innovative-teams/.

world—and if you are open and curious and embracing of those other places, you will know that there is so much innovation and experience outside of just what is in your sphere. You will have the humility to embrace the understanding that your experience or perspective might not be the only way—or the best way—to look at things.

BUILD A DIVERSE TEAM

My experience leading global and diverse teams has taught me that implementing cultural intelligence requires more than good intentions—it demands systematic change and consistent action. We can see this playing out today with the debate around H-1B visas in the United States. Business leaders are fighting for the new administration to allocate more visas to hire top talent, which would help build diversity—but there is strong pushback due to the complex fears around immigration we've discussed in earlier chapters.[90]

But the truth is, if you can overcome those fears and look outside yourself, you will find inspiration and experiences you can learn from. If you have an insular view that your experience is automatically superior, you will be missing out. This is why the Multicultural Mindset is important on an institutional, societal, and national level—but that all begins on the individual level and then ripples outward. If you have a closed mindset that values sameness, conformity, or nationalistic non-multicultural views, you will be at a disadvantage in business in fostering competitive teams for the future. Unfortunately, many managers hire people who are just like them—regardless of what race, ethnicity, or culture the manager belongs to.

---

90   Jake Horton and Bernd Debusmann Jr., "What We Know About US Visas Trump Supporters Are Clashing Over," BBC, December 30, 2024, https://www.bbc.com/news/articles/ckg87n2ml11o.

I've done a lot of hiring, and I've done a lot of firing, and my number one rule has always been to hire people who are smarter than me and not like me. The first is a fairly common mindset (though certainly not everyone practises it!); after all, you're only as good as your weakest team members, so you always want to find people who are better.

But hiring people who are not like me means intentionally seeking to build multicultural teams, which is more challenging—not because there is a lack of multicultural candidates to hire but because of our own internal biases that come into play.

Last year, during a leadership meeting, one of our senior managers expressed frustration about team dynamics. "I just work better with people who think like me," they admitted, referring to people who spoke the same language. A candid moment revealed what researchers call "homophily bias"—our natural tendency to gravitate toward similar people.[91]

In *Tribal*, Michael Morris writes about how we are naturally attracted to people who are from our own tribe because of shared cultural and social cues.[92] We feel people from our own tribe can see us, that we have a point of connection. In the workplace, this can result in managers only hiring people who are like themselves. We can't help it; it's basic human psychology—and it's not a bad thing. It's just something you need to be aware of. If you are aware of it, you can consciously make the decision to hire people who are not like you. Instead of dismissing the senior manager's concern, we used it as an opportunity to examine how unconscious preferences shape our organizational decisions.

---

91   Miller McPherson, Lynn Smith-Lovin, and James M. Cook, "Birds of a Feather: Homophily in Social Networks," *Annual Review of Sociology* 27 (2001): 415–44, https://www.jstor.org/stable/2678628.

92   Morris, *Tribal*.

The transformation began with a simple exercise: mapping our team's decision-making patterns. We discovered that project assignments, promotion recommendations, and even casual lunch groups followed predictable cultural lines.

Rather than implementing mandatory diversity quotas or additional training sessions, we restructured our work processes. Project teams were deliberately configured to cross cultural boundaries. Mentorship pairs were arranged to connect people from different backgrounds. Most importantly, we changed how we measured success—moving beyond representation metrics to track cross-cultural collaboration and innovation outcomes.

This success aligns with what Meyer calls "cultural intelligence in action."[93] It's not enough to understand cultural differences intellectually; organizations must create structures that actively support cross-cultural engagement. The key lies in making these structures feel natural rather than forced—embedding them in daily operations rather than treating them as special initiatives.

Additionally, this is where, with a Multicultural Mindset, leaders can step in and say, "Hey, you may not realize it, but you're doing this, and why don't we think about it this way instead?" People have a tendency to slip back into their patterns of comfort. But the more we call it out and change those practices, the more we can build multicultural teams that are more reflective of the world today. Although this hiring manager was at first offended when I called them out, we did end up hiring a more diverse team, to the benefit of the business.

Today, most workforces are growing in diversity—but not at all levels. It's easy to hire someone outside of your comfort zone if you don't need to interact with them every day. As a leader, you can also

---

93   Erin Meyer, *The Culture Map.*

help negate this by making sure you have diversity at the managerial level so that the people in charge of hiring are themselves diverse.

Go Beyond Checking the Box

Workplace equity and inclusion efforts are well intentioned—but they often result in only surface-level changes. They can make it easy to say, "OK, we hired this percentage of people with X ethnic background. OK, we had a workshop. We can check that box off; no need to worry about it anymore."

But simply having a diverse workforce does not mean you have achieved a Multicultural Mindset in the workplace. Organizations need to put in place values and policies that encourage multiculturalism. DEI initiatives are all well and good, but they only go so far if they're just being used to check a box. Multicultural values need to be lived and seen.

Diversity initiatives certainly have their place and can be very helpful. For example, as a minority woman–led and minority woman–owned business, I'm a certified diverse supplier. There are diversity programs in which large enterprise procurement teams have a quota to meet diverse businesses, and the only way to ensure those businesses are diverse is through certification. We pay a fee each year to maintain AVC's certification, which is a big commitment—but the benefit is that it attracts clients who otherwise may have gone in another direction.

Without diversity programs such as this, I may not have been even considered by some of these clients, especially if I didn't have any personal connection or influence. I am happy to be the benefactor of these programs, because it allows me to get a foot in the door—and then I can start to have a greater influence on increasing multiculturalism from within.

But if you're just checking boxes, you are not reaping the benefits of the Multicultural Mindset. You are not leveraging that diversity, as we discussed in the previous chapter. You have to go deeper. You have to connect with and listen to the perspectives of all these diverse people you've brought into your company. One of the reasons the media planner and account manager were even comfortable sharing their challenges is because we had an environment where they could come to me or to a manager and express themselves. It was a safe place.

It is imperative, when organizations say they support diversity, equity, and inclusion that they actually live it. How do you live it? By articulating openness, respect, and empathy. By making sure everyone's voice really matters. And by having rules and policies in place to ensure these things happen. If you don't put DEI policy front and centre, it becomes invisible. It's not top of mind—and therefore it's usually not being lived.

You have to think it, you have to speak it, and you have to *be* it. And I can tell you from experience, it makes all the difference.

THINK IT, SPEAK IT, BE IT

Recently, AVC hosted a fasting challenge during Ramadan. Twenty percent of my staff are practising Muslims, meaning they all fast during Ramadan. We make accommodations for them to start or end their workday later to allow them to follow their eating and fasting schedule—but I wanted to go further, to go deeper. I wanted to immerse myself in the experience so I could better understand. So, I fasted with them—not for the entire span of Ramadan but for a day. I documented this experience and shared it. And we hosted a big Iftar feast at the end of the day for everyone to participate in, regardless of faith.

Afterward, all of the staff—both Muslim and non-Muslim—said the same thing to me: "It is wonderful that you are not just saying you support us; you are actually walking in our shoes in order to understand us."

Since then, other companies have tried to poach some of my high-talent Muslim staff with some pretty big offers—but they've all said no. What keeps them with me, this small, independent agency in Canada? The affinity and connection they feel—not just with the company but with me, the CEO, who shared in their tradition. How do I know this?

Because they've told me: "I turned down the offer because I want to keep building what we're building together. We know that you are coming from a place of wanting to uplift communities that are under-represented—we can tell by the way you participated in our tradition in order to more deeply understand our culture." I won't lie—I cried when they told me this.

In-House Immersion

Throughout my time at AVC, I've consciously tried to have our company focus more on celebrating each other's cultures, backgrounds, and traditions, beyond the Anglo-Saxon Christian ones generally included in the secular calendar. I've heard so many stories from non-Christian friends and colleagues about their workplaces completely failing to take holidays from other religions into account—scheduling important events on Yom Kippur or Passover or Ramadan or Diwali or Vaisakhi. I wanted AVC to be different.

Like most companies, our company has a holiday party every year for Christmas. One year, I said, "You know what, screw the Christmas party. Half of you take a week off to travel back to China to celebrate Lunar New Year—let's celebrate Lunar New Year. Instead of a Christmas party, let's have a Lunar New Year party!" Our Lunar New Year party was such a great success that I decided we should change it up every year. After all, why should the focus only be on Christian holidays? This past year, we did a Diwali party!

The party was a great experience for two reasons. One, most of the team had never celebrated Lunar New Year with their Chinese teammates. They were aware of it, but they hadn't actually experienced it. Celebrating together brought the team closer—and it was super fun!

Second, it grounded the team in the knowledge of why Lunar New Year is important. Then, when we were talking to clients about Lunar New Year marketing strategies and pitching proposals to brands, we could speak from a more rooted, understanding place, having experienced it ourselves. We could become advocates. That's why I look at the internal events almost like training for the team, during which we learn about these cultural traditions and celebrations by experiencing them firsthand.

In addition to sharing immersive cultural events, you can create workspaces that are actually welcoming of a multicultural workforce. While it may not be realistic to close your office for every single holiday of every single religion, you can make your workplace more accommodating for religions and cultures beyond the Anglo-Saxon Christian holidays that are automatically included in the secular calendar. Check in with your employees about their individual cultural and religious needs and what days they need off for holidays, and don't schedule important all-staff meetings or deadlines for those employees on those days.

In fact, you can create a workspace welcoming of all identities, cultural and otherwise. You can provide bathrooms for all gender identities, flexwork schedules for parents and nursing rooms in the office and prayer rooms for staff. You can have a real impact on people's daily lives. And you can do this outside of work too, advocating for these accommodations in your kids' school, in your local government and in your community.

FROM FETE AND FUSION TO MAINSTREAM

What I've learned from AVC internal events is that the learning and mindset we foster within the company carries over into the work we create for clients. Whether we are doing these events internally for our team or for our clients, there are usually four pillars of connection involved: faith, food, fusion, and fete.

For many events, there is automatically a faith factor—many of these celebrations, including Ramadan, Diwali, and Lunar New Year, are faith-based. There is also almost always a food factor—and we make sure to fully immerse in and enjoy the culturally associated food and drink!

For example, my company recently brought cultural fusion to life for a client, Cadillac Fairview. Cadillac Fairview owns shopping malls all across Canada. For the past five years, the company has thrown elaborate Lunar New Year extravaganzas for the whole community. I love seeing little kids of all backgrounds getting as excited to see the lion dance as they would to see Santa Claus or the Easter Bunny. These kids are already developing a Multicultural Mindset!

One year, for the Lunar New Year celebration at one of the malls, we had a traditional Chinese dance—and we also brought in indigenous Canadian hip-hop artists to play alongside the traditional line dancers. To me, this kind of fusion is essential—because culture is not static. For me, multiculturalism is about embracing the multi—and you can do that while still respecting age-old cultural traditions.

And finally, there is the fete—the party! Many of these cultural events are rooted in celebration. In my experience, the combination of faith, food, fusion, and fete leads to an experience that creates a lasting impression. Every time we've done this, clients want more. Why? Because they see the business impact. They see the stickiness, the engagement it creates with their customers—far beyond what they would get from just running banner ads online.

But these lasting impressions have an impact far beyond businesses. What happens when cultural fetes become fused to mainstream culture?

Did you know that the commercialization of St. Patrick's Day, originally a religious observance honouring Ireland's patron saint, was driven by marketing? Specifically, the marketing of a little beer called Guinness.

Let me go back a bit further. In chapter 4, I mentioned one of my favourite clients: Diageo. When first onboarding our agency to serve Diageo in Canada, I learned more about its history as a company—including, to my surprise and delight, that it was formed in 1997 through the merger of two major companies: Guinness PLC and Grand Metropolitan PLC. Up until that point, Guinness had been a very Irish and deeply cultural brand, founded in 1759 by Arthur Guinness in Dublin, Ireland. Deeply rooted in Irish culture and heritage, Guinness has become a symbol of Ireland, celebrated not only for its beer but also for its contributions to Irish history, economy, and global identity.

To celebrate Irish culture, Guinness launched various advertising campaigns to promote its brand during St. Patrick's Day, which eventually grew to become mainstream mainstays. St. Patrick's Day was a cultural religious festival. Guinness's attachment to the holiday in its marketing helped push St. Patrick's Day into the mainstream. It's part of why St. Patrick's Day parades are now commonplace celebrations.

This has not been without critique, with some critics arguing that the commercialization of St. Patrick's Day perpetuates stereotypes about Irish culture, particularly the association with excessive drinking. There are also concerns that the true meaning of St. Patrick's Day is being lost. The emphasis on beer consumption and branded merchandise often takes precedence over traditional celebrations and the honouring of Irish heritage. And I'm sure there are drinkers of Irish stout who look at Guinness and say, "That's not my beer anymore. They've sold out."

But there's no denying that, today, St. Patrick's Day has evolved into a global celebration characterized by parades, green attire, and public festivities. In the United States, the first St. Patrick's Day parade took place in New York City in 1762, organized by Irish soldiers serving in the British army. Today, it's become completely mainstream.

I believe the commercialization of festivals such as St. Patrick's Day has set a precedent for the next wave of commercialization of culture. Lunar New Year, Diwali, Vaisakhi, and more could be on the horizon next. While the evolution of these cultural events to be more multiculturally mainstream may result in a dilution of the original faith-based significance, it also shows that cultural fusion has been happening all around us, enriching national calendars and fostering cross-cultural appreciation.

Diageo was one of the earliest companies to take a cultural icon— an Irish beer called Guinness—and create a huge brand identity and conglomerate around it, while still maintaining the ties to the beer's cultural roots—but it's not the only one.

Tim Hortons was born in Canada, in Hamilton, Ontario. Now, it is owned by Restaurant Brands International, a huge Brazil-based conglomerate that owns Burger King, Popeyes, and numerous other brands. Today, Tim Hortons has branches all over the world—but no matter where in the world you are, it always displays the Canadian Maple Leaf. It is still distinctly a Canadian brand, tied to Canadian culture. Even though it has gone global, the Canadian aspect of the brand has not been lost or watered down.

What is mainstream will always shift. What was mainstream a generation ago is not mainstream today, and what is mainstream today will not be mainstream a generation from now. And the transition of cultural events and icons from niche to mainstream has only proliferated with technology. Opportunities for the niche to become mainstream have presented themselves faster because of access to information and the viral explosions that can happen on social media. The people, businesses, and brands that can navigate these changes are the ones that will succeed.

One of the most salient truths I've learned during my career is how interconnected we all are. Yet many people still feel underrepresented in their workplaces, in their communities, and in their votes. The autonomy to have and build a Multicultural Mindset that can be a bridge that connects you to others—and celebrates the shared humanity we all have—is the business case.

KEY TAKEAWAYS

→ Learning about different cultural communication styles is essential for fostering cross-cultural understanding—and for understanding ourselves!

→ Implementing a mindset of multiculturalism requires more than good intentions; it requires action and systemic change—which can also mean fun, such as celebrating different cultural events at the office!

→ Multicultural efforts in the workplace can impact the larger world, paving the way for multicultural events to become mainstream.

CHAPTER 8

BETTER TOOLS FOR THE MULTICULTURAL ERA

"Like all living systems, cultures cannot remain static;
they evolve or decline. They explore or expire."

—Buzz Aldrin

*W*hen I first started exploring AI tools, I asked ChatGPT to explain Filipino culture. Its response was so generic, it reminded me of my sixth-grade "Share Your Culture" project—minus the traumatic bubble tea experience!

In today's rapidly evolving digital landscape, humans and technology are engaging in an unprecedented dance of adaptation. Eighty-five percent of jobs that will exist in 2030 haven't been invented yet[94]—and I'm willing to bet that most of them will require both technological and cultural intelligence.

---

94 "Realizing 2030: Dell Technologies Research Explores the Next Era of Human-Machine Partnerships," Dell Technologies, 2017, https://www.dell.com/en-us/dt/corporate/newsroom/realizing-2030-dell-technologies-research-explores-the-next-era-of-human-machine-partnerships.htm.

The challenge isn't just technological—it's deeply human.

Think about this: Can a voice-activated AI recognize a command said in a Punjabi accent or a Scottish accent or a Filipino accent? My uncle tries to talk to Google's chatbot assistant in his Filipino accent, and it does not recognize his voice. His solution? Speaking s-l-o-w-e-r and LOUDER—because obviously, that's how technology works, right? (Spoiler alert: It isn't, but watching him try is comedy gold!)

DATA DIVERSITY IMPERATIVE

As the AI Era collides with the Multicultural Era, the Multicultural Mindset is a necessity in the formation of the systems driving AI modelling and training. The fact is, humans are inherently biased. There are things we like and don't like. There may even be names we like and don't like because of the associations we have with them! AI can help eliminate those unconscious biases—but only if the AI itself is unbiased.

AI is revolutionizing many industries. Big data is driving much of the business and marketing industry today. We have platforms to analyze data. We have other tools to collate and organize data. And now, we have super AI tools to do virtually everything involving data. But here's the uncomfortable truth: It's riddled with bias.

Consider these scenarios:

- Voice recognition systems may have difficulty recognizing or have high error rates for non-native English speakers.

- Facial recognition algorithms may demonstrate disparities for certain ethnic groups.

- Language processing models exhibit significant bias in content generation for different cultural contexts.

When the data points are not diverse, when they are not representative, it presents a problem for the industry at large. You end up with what is known as garbage in, garbage out—meaning, if bad data or flawed inputs go into the system, you'll get bad results or outputs no matter how advanced the system is.[95]

If AI is the future, it needs to represent the diversity of reality—which means we need to make sure we are inputting diverse thoughts, opinions, perspectives, and data. We can't let human biases fuel the AI systems of our future industry.

This can only be done with increased representation at the foundational level. This is the only way to build responsible AI that is inclusive and truly multicultural. AI systems must be built with multicultural intelligence and inclusion at their core. From content generation to audience targeting, brands and agencies can play a role in creating, training, and monitoring AI tools to prevent biased outcomes.

There are already people and companies out there making this effort, working to reframe the source data and doing so in an IRL way. For example, Pocstock is a global media company specializing in providing authentic, royalty-free stock photos, videos, and illustrations that prominently feature people of colour. Their extensive library includes images of Black, Hispanic, Asian, Indigenous, BIPOC, LGBTQIA+, and disabled individuals, aiming to offer positive and diverse representations built through IRL engagement with the community.[96]

---

95   Ron Ozminkowski, "Garbage In, Garbage Out," *Towards Data Science* (blog), November 16, 2021, https://medium.com/towards-data-science/garbage-in-garbage-out-721b5b299bc1.

96   Samantha Dorisca, "Black-Led Pocstock Raises $500K in a Seed Funding Round," Yahoo Finance, October 27, 2023, https://finance.yahoo.com/news/black-led-pocstock-raises-500k-164632994.html.

Experience and immersion, the foundational inputs of a Multicultural Mindset, are also what provide the good data with which to create good AI. The fact is, getting away from technology is going to make technology better. Someone who has been immersed in the real world, building their Multicultural Mindset, is going to create better AI than someone who has been isolated in their own bubble.

Building Multicultural Tools

The role of the Multicultural Mindset in the future of technology is to ensure responsible AI that is inclusive and unbiased—and holding the companies that build these tools responsible for accurately reflecting the multicultural world.

In a recent analysis of Google's Gemini chatbot and OpenAI's ChatGPT, The Culture Factor Group found that "while both Gemini and ChatGPT demonstrate the potential to mimic human conversation accurately, their ability to grasp the subtle intricacies of culture is severely lacking."[97] This happens because product designers and engineers are not creating products with inclusion in mind.

This is true not just for AI tools but for all technologies. Think about writing a document in Microsoft Word. Just a few years ago, if you typed the name Gupta or Singh or pretty much any ethnic name, you would see a little red "incorrect spelling" line under the name. This probably would have remained true today—if it weren't for a campaign by Elimin8Hate, the advocacy arm of the Vancouver Asian Film Festival.

In 2022, Elimin8Hate developed "the world's first custom dictionary plug-in, ReclaimYourName.dic, of over 8,000 Asian names

---

97 "Gemini vs ChatGPT: Which AI Wins the Cultural Understanding Challenge," The Culture Factor Group, accessed December 30, 2024, https://www.theculturefactor.com/gemini-vs-chatgpt.

that removes the red underline marking it a typo, in partnership with Citizen Relations." In 2023, the initiative was "recognized by Microsoft and is being added into current and future Microsoft 365 application updates, including Microsoft Word."[98]

The software needed to be built inclusively from the root level—and as we've discussed, you can't successfully build something for someone unless you include them in the building process.

There are some other examples of multicultural technologies out there, built by and for multicultural audiences. For example, there's BLACKGPT, which is like ChatGPT but from a Black culture point of view, trained by Black people, for Black people. But a few years ago, I noticed that there aren't a lot of tools out there specifically to aid with multicultural marketing.

So, I decided to build one myself.

DON'T WAIT TULONG

Marketing technology (MarTech) is a booming industry. It is set to exceed $217 billion USD by 2027[99]—and yet there's no proliferation or commensurate growth of tools addressing representation and diversity. So, in 2023, I founded my own MarTech company and filed two patents to protect the ideas we were putting forward.

It was this gap that inspired the formation of my start-up company, TULONG Technologies, with the mission of revolutionizing multicultural marketing technology and becoming the world's

---

98 "Citizen Custom Dictionary Makes Fast Company's World Changing Ideas 2023 List, Gets Implemented by Microsoft," Citizen Relations, May 30, 2023, https://www.citizenrelations.com/en/citizen-custom-dictionary-makes-fast-companys-world-changing-ideas-2023-list-gets-implemented/.

99 Chris Wood, "MarTech Set to Exceed $215 Billion by 2027," MarTech, January 23, 2024, https://martech.org/martech-set-to-exceed-215-billion-by-2027/.

leading provider of multicultural marketing solutions. Choosing the Filipino word for "help" wasn't only about heritage; it was also about addressing a fundamental need in the industry. I also liked that the word sounds like "too long"—because let's not wait too long before building tools to address this growing multicultural population, this growing investable and addressable market that is right in front of us!

I positioned TULONG as a MarTech start-up focused on business-to-business software as a solution (B2B SaaS). I focused on B2B to connect with the marketing industry rather than a consumer solution, because that is the industry I serve today and the one I have a direct pipeline to—and it's the one that has been the most archaic and stuck in tunnel vision as an industry.

My digital media team compiles data across every audience and campaign we execute for brands globally and conducts an annual digital benchmarks study. In our presentation of the data to The Interactive Advertising Bureau of Canada, the leading organization on digital marketing and media globally, we shared performance indicators of multicultural marketing campaigns for which results were two times better than mainstream corresponding key performance indicators.[100] Yet most marketers struggle to find support to launch integrated multicultural engagement campaigns, as the attribution and tools across the marketing ecosystem are nascent.

Our journey with TULONG revealed something surprising: The problem isn't just about technology—it is about access and transparency. Traditional media buying often operates through what industry analysts call "relationship privilege," where access to diverse media channels depends heavily on existing networks and connections.

---

100 "Reaching a Diverse Canadian Market: Multicultural Digital Benchmark Study," AVCommunications, 2021, https://iabcanada.com/wp-content/uploads/2021/07/ IAB-Digital-Benchmarks-Deck_AVC_FINAL.pdf.

The solution emerged through creating what I like to call a "democratic marketplace" for multicultural media. By bringing together over one thousand publishers across different cultural contexts, TULONG's platform provides marketers with transparent access to diverse media options, allowing their campaign strategies to naturally become more inclusive.

It took two years for me to bring TULONG to life—and it was not an easy road! First of all, while I have seen more focus lately in the tech space on trying to get more diverse investors to invest in more diverse businesses, when I was pitching TULONG to venture capital firms, I encountered so many people who just didn't get it.

"Why do we need a tool like this?" they asked. "Why is this a problem we need to address?"

Since the majority of the investment community is from cultures that are not generally underrepresented in marketing,[101] they hadn't experienced this problem themselves, and therefore our pitch often fell on deaf ears. The people who got it right away were all people from underrepresented communities—and they all said, "Oh, yeah, we definitely need that."

I also learned quickly that tech companies with high valuations can fail really, really easily if the valuation is too puffed up and not rooted in reality. So, I set out early to bootstrap TULONG, knowing it was a complete gamble—but knowing I was gambling on myself, what I knew, and what I could bring to the table. So, it wasn't really a gamble; it was an investment.

---

101   Suraj Gupta, "Diversity: The Holy Grail of Venture Capital," *Forbes*, May 26, 2022, https://www.forbes.com/councils/forbesbusinesscouncil/2022/05/26/diversity-the-holy-grail-of-venture-capital/.

A Multicultural Media Marketplace–Patent Pending!

On TULONG, we have two services: media planning and creative solutions. At its most basic level, marketing consists of a message on some kind of media. Say I'm a busy marketer representing a brand and I want to reach out to diverse audiences. My first stops for media would probably be Google, Facebook, Amazon, TikTok, etc.—which are great, but I'm missing out on the rich inventory of Hotstar, Jio, and Globoplay—all these other in-language international and ethnic media channels that are available but not visible to the market.

You can only book what you know, which means more dollars go to the platforms that everyone knows: Google, Facebook, etc. But local and culturally specific media is where more diverse voices get nurtured—and where you can reach those audiences.

TULONG puts all of that inventory in one place: a marketplace of media channels. As of now, we have over a thousand different publishers and thousands of different formats available. Users can look through this marketplace and say, "I didn't know there was a radio station in this language! Let's market there to reach that audience!"

This same service from a consultancy firm would mean having a discovery meeting, doing a briefing, waiting for a plan that could take hundreds of hours and then waiting for someone to present that plan—it all takes too long! With TULONG, users can browse and book right from their phone.

It's like Airbnb for media platforms. You can browse and search, and you can get AI algorithm recommendations based on your searches and use. Right now, you can submit a manual booking order to a customer success manager on the back end; eventually, that will be automated as well—we're still working on building all the railroad tracks behind the scenes.

Every user who has tried TULONG so far has said the same thing: "This saved me so much time!" Instead of having to search for all these individual media platforms and figure out how to book on each one, you can just use this one marketplace to do it all.

THE MEDIUM IS STILL THE MESSAGE

The future of technology and the future of AI, whether it becomes a boon or a detriment, comes down to the stewardship and governance required to ensure ethical use of the tool.

The advent of the internet represented a move away from regulation of the media. The premise of my master's thesis, "Marketing of Culture, Hybridity, and Identity in Virtual Spaces: A Virtual Ethnography," was that the internet was creating new communities and new senses of identity. We were no longer limited to our geographic location; we could now be part of a community on the other side of the world, with people from all over the world, built around a shared interest or culture. It was meant to create a greater sense of connection, a greater sense of understanding and knowledge—and to a certain extent, it did.

But the new medium of the internet didn't come with the same governance and stewardship as radio or TV, which had ratings systems and such. Sure, there's YouTube Kids. Sure, you have to put in your age before you enter certain sites—but that doesn't do much. By the time kids today are thirteen years old, if they have access to Wi-Fi, they have probably seen pornography.[102]

---

102 Pranujan Pathmendra et al., "Exposure to Pornography and Adolescent Sexual Behavior: Systematic Review," *Journal of Medical Internet Research* 25 (February 28, 2023), https://doi.org/10.2196/43116.

As Canadian communication theorist Marshall McLuhan put it, "The medium is the message." In his book *Understanding Media: The Extensions of Man* (in which the first chapter is titled "The Medium is the Message"), McLuhan writes about the impact the mediums of radio and TV have on society and psychology.[103] When McLuhan wrote *Understanding Media* in 1964, he couldn't have predicted the rise of AI, yet his insights about how media shapes human consciousness proved remarkably prescient for our current technological revolution. As we navigate the intersection of AI and cultural intelligence, his famous observation that "the medium is the message" takes on new significance.

McLuhan himself, even though he was an artist, was very pro-regulation and adamant that society needs structure. But AI doesn't have that structure. After all, how can you regulate a prompt? AI is often programmed with protections in place, trained to not answer these kinds of questions, but people have easily found workarounds. When the algorithm or a chatbot is dictating what you're seeing and reading, when it has the ability to move the human condition toward something impactful, it can very quickly go bad. This is when governance and ethical guidelines around the use of AI become so important.

Much has been written and studied about the dangers of social media and technology, including its impact on psychology, so we won't dive into it more here—that's a subject for another book! (But if you're interested in that topic, the documentaries *The Social Dilemma* or *What's Next with Bill Gates* are great places to start!)

---

103 Marshall McLuhan, *Understanding Media: The Extensions of Man* (McGraw-Hill, 1964).

MOST INFLUENTIAL FILIPINAS IN THE WORLD

In 2022, I had the honour of being named by the Filipina Women's Network as one of the Most Influential Filipinas in the world. The award was humbling but also mind-blowing, as previous recipients included 2021 Nobel Peace Prize winner Maria Ressa.

Like McLuhan, Ressa offers warnings about technology and human connection—warnings given extra weight by her remarkable life story. Ressa is cofounder of Rappler, the Philippines' leading independent news platform and one of the country's first online-only news sites. With over thirty years of journalism experience, Ressa has always been committed to the truth—which often came at a steep personal cost.

Under the oppressive regime of President Rodrigo Duterte, Ressa's fight against disinformation and cyber harassment led to multiple arrests and cyber libel charges—and a deep understanding of how digital platforms can be weaponized.

The Nobel Committee recognized Ressa's fight by awarding her the 2021 Peace Prize (shared with Russian journalist Dmitry Muratov), citing her "efforts to safeguard freedom of expression, which is a precondition for democracy and lasting peace."[104] She became the first Filipino Nobel laureate—and brought global attention to the fight for freedom of the press in the digital age.

In her powerful book *How to Stand Up to a Dictator*, Ressa warns us about technology's potential to reshape not only how we communicate but also how we connect as human beings. "The absence of rule of law in the virtual world is devastating," she writes.[105]

---

104 "Nobel Peace Prize 2021," The Nobel Prize, October 8, 2021, https://www.nobelprize.org/prizes/peace/2021/press-release/.

105 Maria Ressa, *How to Stand Up to a Dictator: The Fight for Our Future*, 1st edition (Harper, 2022).

As we move forward in this rapidly evolving landscape, our north star must be the Multicultural Mindset—an approach that embraces both technological advancement and human connection. This mindset recognizes that while AI can help us bridge cultural gaps, it's our human capacity for empathy, understanding, and genuine connection that will ultimately determine how successfully we navigate our increasingly multicultural world.

The Multicultural Mindset is about wanting to understand people. It goes beyond work. It even goes beyond culture. At its core, the Multicultural Mindset is about human interaction. Because at the deepest level, we are all just human; we are all oscillating, moving through life at the speed of culture.

KEY TAKEAWAYS

→ AI can only be an effective tool in the Multicultural Era if the data it is trained on reflects the diversity of reality.

→ There are multiculturally focused technologies out there—including my own TULONG multicultural media marketplace!

→ The dangers of AI are great—but so are the opportunities, if it is safeguarded with regulations and built with a Multicultural Mindset.

CONCLUSION

Remember that little Filipina girl out in the prairies of northern Alberta? She could never have imagined the world we live in today—how technology has transformed the way we connect, communicate, work, and live. But she would still recognize one fundamental thing that hasn't changed and never will: the power of human connection, across borders, across cultures.

Harnessing this power in today's Multicultural Era is what developing a Multicultural Mindset is all about. It's not just a business strategy; it's a way of being. Throughout this book, we've explored how we can push beyond superficial diversity initiatives and into authentic cultural immersion, leading to lasting transformation. We've seen how cross-cultural communication can open us up to new levels of understanding, how we can overcome our cultural inertia, how we can go deeper than surface level—and all the benefits this brings, both in business and in life.

A LETTER TO THE FUTURE

Remember during the first year of the pandemic, when video calls went from being fairly unusual to being completely mainstream? It was definitely a learning curve; my mom yelled into the phone even though she was on video! "Ma! I can see you! You don't need to shout," I replied. But you know what? Even with the awkward camera angles of her forehead and the occasional frozen screen, those calls kept us connected. That's the thing about technology—it's not about perfection; it's about possibility.

To whoever is reading this (maybe even with the help of some yet-to-be-invented AI assistant!):

Your world probably looks different from mine—just as my world now looks different from the world of my childhood. Maybe we no longer have to rely on Zoom to talk to distant friends and family— maybe we'll be able to teleport instantly! Maybe a voice-activated chatbot will finally be able to understand my uncle's accent. Maybe we'll have invented a device that can digitally transmit the smell of freshly cooked rice (if so, please forward me the patent royalties!)

But I bet some things haven't changed:

- The warmth of seeing someone smile as you enjoy the food of their culture

- The joy of finding connection despite our differences

- The excitement when you suddenly see something from another perspective

- The human need—a need that will never disappear—for real, deep, authentic connection

Your Multicultural Toolkit

As you navigate the ever-evolving landscape of our ever-changing world, there are things to remember:

- Your Multicultural Mindset provides your unshakeable foundation.

- Your MQ is your GPS.

- Technology can amplify your Mindset and MQ—if used conscientiously.

- The goal should always be more human connection, not less.

- Stay curious, keep learning, and keep exploring!

- Always try that one unfamiliar dish at the office potluck (well, except maybe balut—you might want to work up to that one!).

The Last Byte

Marshall McLuhen, Maria Ressa, and many others have warned us about technology's power to reshape human connection. They're right about this power—but I believe we get to choose *how* that power reshapes us. Every day, we should ask ourselves these questions:

- Am I building bridges or walls—connecting or dividing?

- Am I deepening or replacing human connection?

- Am I expanding or limiting my understanding?

In the end, it's not a choice between technology and human connection—it's about whether, and *how*, one can enhance the other.

As you close this book and pick up your phone (although let's be real, it's probably been in your hand the whole time!), remember: You're part of a bigger picture. It's a brave new world—and as you navigate cultures and technology, you are helping to shape how we connect with one another.

A Brighter Future

Recently, I was at a resort in Mexico for an AVC corporate team retreat. The director of operations of the resort was a Mayan Mexican man with a very international and multicultural family. He shared with me that he has a sister who lives in Canada and a brother who lives in the US and that his family network includes Jewish, African, Mexican, and Filipino members.

"My family is diverse and beautiful," he told me, "so this is all I know. And when I see kids come and play here at the resort, I see that they don't know bias. Kids say, 'Hey, come and play, let's be friends!' no matter who you are or what you look like or if you even speak the same language. And I wonder: Why is it, when we become adults, our guards come up and our labels come on, and we can't just play at the park together anymore?"

As we talked, I watched the kids playing in the pool—kids from all over the world. "We lose our inner child," the director said, following my gaze. "We lose something. We need to capture that again."

His words struck my heart because I couldn't agree more. No matter what the future holds, we need to recapture our unbiased inner children, who greet each other with trust and a smile—and we can do that by measuring and improving our Multicultural Mindset.

The future belongs to those with high MQ and an always-on Multicultural Mindset. Understanding that cultural intelligence can't be downloaded but must be developed will ensure the best interfaces are still smiles and the strongest networks are built on trust.

Welcome to the Multicultural Era.

With hope for our shared inclusive future,

Jacelyn David

ABOUT THE AUTHOR

Joycelyn David is an award-winning business leader, entrepreneur, and advocate for multicultural marketing and BIPOC creatives. As the CEO of AVC, a leading full-service multicultural marketing agency and the only Filipina-owned firm of its kind in Canada, Joycelyn has led the company to remarkable success. Since acquiring AVC in 2019, she has driven its rapid growth across North America, working with major clients such as BMO Financial, Canon, Diageo Canada, and the government of Ontario. Under her leadership, AVC earned a coveted spot on *The Globe and Mail*'s list of Canada's Top Growing Companies, ranking No. 268 with a three-year growth of 154 percent.

Beyond her business acumen, Joycelyn is a dedicated community leader and advocate. In 2022, she was named one of the Most Influential Filipinas in the World, joining the ranks of Toronto-based trailblazers such as Honourable Minister Rechie Valdez and Dr. Eileen de Villa. She also serves as secretary and board member of POCAM, furthering her commitment to diversity and representation in the industry.

With over two decades of global experience, Joycelyn is a sought-after speaker, frequently presenting at major conferences and summits, including *The Globe and Mail* Top Growth Summit, BCAMA, IAB Canada, and Digital Marketing for Financial Services. Drawing from her insights and expertise, she is now channelling her knowledge into an upcoming book that promises to inspire and empower future leaders.

When she's not leading AVC or speaking on industry stages, Joycelyn invests her time and resources into fostering BIPOC talent in film, music, and other creative arts. With multiple movie credits to her name, she continues to champion diverse voices in the entertainment industry. Based in Toronto, she enjoys life with her husband Abraham and son Lorenzo, balancing her passion for business, creativity, and community impact.

CONTACT

Want to continue the conversation? Connect with me and AVC by scanning this link:

www.ingramcontent.com/pod-product-compliance
Lightning Source LLC
Chambersburg PA
CBHW031432270326
41930CB00007B/673